PLATE 1   BOSCOBEL RESTORATION, GARRISON-ON-HUDSON   NO. 9 ON MAP
PUTNAM COUNTY: FRONT FACADE

Historic Houses

of

The Hudson Valley

by

HAROLD DONALDSON EBERLEIN

and

CORTLANDT VAN DYKE HUBBARD

Sponsored by

The Hudson River Conservation Society, Inc.

DOVER PUBLICATIONS, INC., NEW YORK

To

AILEEN OSBORN WEBB

Whose whole-hearted support greatly aided
the publication of this book

Published in Canada by General Publishing Company, Ltd.,
30 Lesmill Road, Don Mills, Toronto, Ontario.

This Dover edition, first published in 1990, is an unabridged
republication of the edition originally published by Architectural
Book Publishing Company, Inc., in 1942, as reprinted with slight
alterations by Bonanza Books, New York, n.d.

Manufactured in the United States of America
Dover Publications, Inc., 31 East 2nd Street, Mineola, N.Y. 11501

Library of Congress Cataloging-in-Publication Data

Eberlein, Harold Donaldson.
Historic houses of the Hudson Valley / Harold Donaldson Eberlein
and Cortlandt Van Dyke Hubbard.
p.   cm.
Reprint. Originally published: New York : Architectural Book Pub. Co., 1942.
ISBN 0-486-26304-5
1. Dwellings—Hudson River Valley (N.Y. and N.J.) 2. Dwellings—
Hudson River Valley (N.Y. and N.J.)—Pictorial works. 3. Historic
buildings—Hudson River Valley (N.Y. and N.J.) 4. Historic
buildings—Hudson River Valley (N.Y. and N.J.)—Pictorial works.
5. Architecture, Domestic—Hudson River Valley (N.Y. and N.J.)
6. Architecture, Domestic—Hudson River Valley (N.Y. and N.J.)—
Pictorial Works. 7. Hudson River Valley (N.Y. and N.J.)—History,
Local. 8. Hudson River Valley (N.Y. and N.J.)—Description and
travel—Views. I. Hubbard, Cortlandt Van Dyke. II. Title.
F127.H8E18   1990
974.7'3—dc 20   89-25884
CIP

CONTENTS

FOREWORD

OLD HOUSES and public edifices are symbols of history, tangible evidences of the past. Like finger-posts, they clearly fix sites of former happenings. As settings for bygone men and deeds, they help us to visualise momentous acts and diverting incidents alike. Through force of association they make history *real* and alive. If you stand in the garden of Fort Crailo and hear that a young officer of General Abercrombie's staff wrote "Yankee Doodle," sitting there on the well-kerb, you would always remember place and incident together. Coming from the windows of a grey old house in Kingston you seem to hear the strains of Aaron Burr's fiddle; the headquarters at Newburgh recall Washington bartering army salt for his breakfast eggs; at Clermont, beside the ruins of Arryl House, the festivities for la Fayette rise before you almost unbidden. The house is always the mordant to fix the story.

The Hudson Valley holds a wealth of history. That history is inseparably bound up with the old *houses* on both sides of the river; without the houses and marked sites of important events, the history would lose its dramatic reality and be a vague abstraction.

The river was the natural, for a long time the only, artery of communication and traffic. To penetrate into the heart of the country the early colonists followed the waterways debouching into the Hudson, as far as they could go by sloop or canoe—after that, on foot along the banks. At the mouths and along the courses of these streams, therefore, you look for many of the earliest settlements. These tributaries offered another inducement to which the pioneers were not blind—abundant water power for mills, and mills were the nuclei of colonisation. The mill was a centre of distribution whither all had to go for the wherewithal for their daily bread. Oftentimes, until a church was established in the neighbourhood, people had no place else to go when they stirred from home; after a church was built, it was a common saying that thenceforth they had *two* places to go—"*to mill and to meetin'.*" The miller did a thriving business as fur trader and general-storekeeper; the mill was the hub of local commerce. Although early roads of indifferent sort had appeared here and there between neighbouring settlements—usually made by widening Indian trails—it was not until the dawn of the 18th century that there was any attempt at road-making for the benefit of the whole Province. Even after improved roads were built, the river long remained the chief highway; "*traders followed it and settlers kept near its waters.*"

The Province's main highway in the days of its beginnings, the Hudson was also the chief line of strategy during the War for Independence. It was the British aim to control the whole length of the river and thus cut off New England from the Middle Colonies and the South. It was Washington's aim to control it and thus keep open an interior line of communication, whatever might befall along the seaboard. Hence the stirring incidents of the struggle along the Hudson's shores.

The houses and estates of the Hudson Valley reflect a system, social and economic which, however much one may approve or disapprove it on general principles and judged by modern standards, profoundly affected the subsequent development of the State. Whatever flaws the doctrinaire democrat may pick in it, the manorial system unquestionably made for strength and stability in the early days of colonisation. It was not a one-sided scheme devised for the sole pleasure and profit of great landowners. It was a system based on the mutual interest of great and lowly alike, the common profit of landlord and tenant, a system of amicable co-operation, and for the advantages each derived he had to render a substantial *quid pro quo*. A social order so deeply rooted during the Colonial period could hardly be swept aside in its entirety by the political upheaval of the Revolution; much of the former manner of life, with its gracious amplitude, lingered on into the early 19th century, retaining old traditions of hospitality and cherishing its closely-knit web of relationships and hereditary friendships. There is as much variety in the architecture of Hudson Valley houses as there is in the history they enshrine or the divers social conditions that gave them birth.

To all who have so helpfully contributed data and extended innumerable other courtesies, the authors wish to express sincere thanks and appreciation; lack of space unfortunately prevents naming them specifically. Unfortunately, too, lack of available space precludes adequate historical consideration of many of the houses illustrated. The authors here desire to acknowledge their indebtedness to Miss Reynolds's invaluable books, and to the staffs of the Historical Society of Pennsylvania, the New York Historical Society and the New York Public Library.

HAROLD DONALDSON EBERLEIN,
CORTLANDT VAN DYKE HUBBARD.

Philadelphia,
April, 1942.

WESTCHESTER COUNTY

FREDERICK PHILIPSE, first Lord of the Manor of Philipsborough, was a conspicuous instance of the industrious, diligent and capable grantee. Scion of a noble Bohemian family that had sought asylum in the Netherlands two generations earlier, as a young man of but slender means he came to New Amsterdam some time prior to 1653. He soon became "carpenter" to the West India Company, charged with supervision of the Company's buildings then in use, and also the planning and erection of their new structures, along with oversight of any public works undertaken by them. Although we have no evidence to prove it, it is likely that Philipse had some architectural training in Holland.

In 1657 he acquired the Small Burgher Right of New Amsterdam; thus he was eligible to hold minor public offices and had the right of trading. Thence onward, apparently backed by the Governour's favour, his progress was rapid. Gradually, but steadily, he bought houses, town lots and other real estate holdings and made judicious investments. Besides his numerous dealings in real estate, he launched forth into various branches of trade until

"his commerce extended to Esopus and Albany on the north and to the South or Delaware River, on the south."

Under both Dutch and English *régimes* Philipse held divers responsibilities and honours. Because of the general trust Government and people alike reposed in him, during Leisler's Rebellion the Governour's Council desired the Government funds placed in Philipse's strong-boxes for safe-keeping. He was a member of the Provincial Council under both Governours Dongan and Fletcher.

In 1672, with two partners, Philipse bought a large part of the old Yonkers Plantation, formerly the Patroonship of Colen Donck. All of this interest he subsequently acquired. To this he added other extensive purchases until his lands reached from Spuyten Duyvil Creek northward to the Croton River—about 22 miles along the east bank of the Hudson. Thus grew the estate that became the Manor of Philipsborough, by Royal Charter, in June, 1693. At the mouth of the Neperhan, where Yonkers now stands, Van der Donck had built a mill. Nearby, Philipse established his residence.

What is now the MANOR HOUSE (Plate 2) seems to have been built not later than 1682; it may have been earlier. Philipse also built a mill at the mouth of the Pocantico, near Tarrytown; there, about 1683, he built another house, now known as Castle Philipse. The house at Neperhan, however, was always his chief place of residence when not in New York City. Philipse often referred to the Yonkers house as the "Lower Mills," the Pocantico settle-

ment as the "Upper Mills." The Manor House in Frederick Philipse's day consisted of the present southern end of the building. There can be little doubt that Philipse designed it himself. At that time it was unquestionably one of the most distinguished examples of domestic architecture in the American Colonies.

In 1691, Margaret Hardenbrook, Frederick Philipse's first wife died. In 1692 he married again, taking to wife Catharine Van Cortlandt, the widow of John Derval.

"She was," we are told, "young and pretty, had a sweet disposition and charming manner, and soon ingratiated herself with the tenants of the great Philipse estate by her generous benevolence."

She it was, in all likelihood, who influenced her husband to what appears to have been their joint undertaking—the building of SLEEPY HOLLOW CHURCH (Plate 16) in 1699. By the same royal charter that created Philipse's lands the "Lordship and Manor of Philipsborough," the Lord of the Manor acquired the right to build across Spuyten Duyvil Creek a toll-bridge, to be called "King's Bridge," and to levy a fee upon everyone using it. The old schedule of tolls is still preserved. With the income from this valuable concession, and his revenue from investments and other sources, Frederick Philipse's fortunes throve apace and were reflected in the ample mode of life at the Manor House, over which Catharine Van Cortlandt presided with genial grace. Recording the elaborate hospitality dispensed there, Dr. Edward Hagaman Hall writes that in summer

"Governours and their satellites and the leading citizens of New York, gayly attired, might have been seen riding a-horseback along the old Post Road . . . bound for the country home of the First Lord."

Frederick Philipse died in 1703 and his seven-year-old grandson Frederick fell heir to the vast Manor estate. Left an orphan in infancy, the terms of his grandfather's will entrusted him to the upbringing of his step-grandmother, Catharine Van Cortlandt. The educational facilities then offered by New York may or may not have been as good as *"these parts of ye world will afford"*; they were not, to Madame Philipse's thinking, of a sort likely to fit her grandson to fill creditably his station in life as Lord of the Manor of Philipsborough. So she took him to England, where he could be educated in a becoming manner. There young Frederick studied law and became imbued with *"the best traditions of his day."* Coming of age in 1716, three years later he married Joanna, daughter of Lieutenant-Governour Brockholls. A more genial and cultured atmosphere now pervaded the Manor House. In marked contrast to

PLATE 2   PHILIPSE MANOR HOUSE, YONKERS: SOUTH DOOR   NO. 1 ON MAP

PLATE 3   PHILIPSE MANOR HOUSE, YONKERS: SOUTH FRONT

PLATE 4   PHILIPSE MANOR HOUSE, YONKERS: EAST AND SOUTH FRONTS

his grandfather, the second Lord of the Manor had strongly developed social inclinations and none of the painful reticence and shyness of the first Lord. Intellectually a man of distinguished parts, he was affable and a good conversationalist; his engaging personality and companionable qualities won him hosts of friends and the esteem of all with whom he came in contact. Nor was the mistress of the house less estimable than the master.

Frederick, the second Lord, played an active rôle in the public life of the Province; he was a Justice of the Peace, for fourteen successive years re-elected an Alderman of the City of New York, and a member of the Provincial Assembly for Westchester County. From 1721 to 1728 he was Speaker of the Assembly. In 1733 he became Provincial Treasurer; the same year, during the Chief-Justiceship of the Honourable James De Lancey, he was appointed Second Judge of the Supreme Court, a dignity he held for the rest of his life.

In 1745 he enlarged the Manor House by a brick addition much greater than the original building, making the eastern side the principal front. Some of the fixed interior decoration of the original part of the house was apparently altered and enriched at the time of the 1745 addition. One of these embellishments consisted of intricate plasterwork on some of the ceilings—scrolls, arabesques, musical instruments, wreaths, mythological figures and medallions containing heads, some of which are said to be likenesses of members of the Philipse family. Between the east front of the house and the Post Road was the garden, the borders edged with low-growing box and filled with choice flowers. So long as the Philipse family remained in the Manor House, the garden was an object of solicitude. There was every opportunity for endless and lavish hospitality; the performance did not lag behind the opportunity. Besides the many guests who sought the master and mistress, the daughters of the house attracted an host

PLATE 6   LIVINGSTON HOUSE, DOBBS'S FERRY: HALL AND STAIR   No. 2 ON MAP

PLATE 7   LIVINGSTON HOUSE, DOBBS'S FERRY: WEST FRONT

of friends and suitors. One of these was Colonel Beverley Robinson, who married the eldest daughter, Susannah.

Frederick Philipse died in 1751, at the age of fifty-six, deeply regretted and highly esteemed by his contemporaries. His son Frederick, third and last Lord of the Manor, succeeded him. A man of literary tastes and domestic inclinations, the third Frederick was more disposed to the management of his estate than to mixing in public affairs. Nevertheless, he held a commission as Colonel of Militia, and was generally known as "Colonel" Philipse to distinguish him from his father, the "Judge." He was also a member of the Provincial Assembly. The Court Leet and Court Baron of the Manor were held in a building near the Manor House; over these he commonly presided in person. In 1765 he married Elizabeth Williams, the young widow of Anthony Rutgers and daughter of Charles Williams, Naval Officer for the Port of New York. The bride was a *"handsome and Pleasing woman,"* according to the clerical estimate of Timothy Dwight. "Handsome" and "excellent," she was also vivacious and dashing, and seems to have had a well-earned reputation as a fearless and skillful horsewoman. Colonel and Mrs. Philipse rarely appeared together in the same carriage—for a very good reason. The Colonel was very fat and, in time, attained such dimensions that *"there was not room enough for both in the family chariot."* Mrs. Philipse's manner of driving, too, may have had something to do with this habit of each "going it alone." Colonel Philipse and his family were staunch and generous Church of England people. They built St. John's Church in Yonkers, a substantial stone building dating from 1752, and met the greater part of the parish expenses at their own charge. Besides, they built a rectory and gave 250 acres of arable land for a glebe.

PLATE 8   LIVINGSTON HOUSE, DOBBS'S FERRY: SOUTH OR GARDEN FRONT

Mary Philipse, Frederick's second sister, had remained single till after her father's death and her brother's marriage. Washington had once shown an ardent attachment for her, but Roger Morris had successfully wooed and won her. Their wedding took place at the Manor House, January 19, 1758. It was not only one of the great social events of the Province that brought together an assemblage of the foremost families and the officers of the British Army; it was also an occasion of high festivity for all the manor tenantry, for whom a bountiful feast was set. The crowds in the parlours shone with all the sumptuous and gaily-coloured raiment of the mid-18th century. After Mary Philipse and Roger Morris had entered, attended by bridesmaids and groomsmen, the marriage service took place under a crimson canopy bearing the family crest in gold—a demi-lion crowned issuing from a coronet. The Lord of the Manor, wearing the gold chain and

jewelled insignia of the ancestral office of Master Ranger of the Royal Forests of Bohemia, gave his sister away.

When the struggle with the Mother Country became acute, men of weight and position could no longer fail to declare their attitude. Colonel Philipse saw his duty in loyalty to the established Government, however much he might personally disapprove measures he believed mistaken. When the Westchester County Whigs met at White Plains, in April, 1778, to elect representatives to the next Continental Congress, the Loyalists also held a meeting there and declared their adherence to Crown and Constitution. This declaration 312 men signed; Colonel Philipse, then a member of the Provincial Assembly, was the first to sign. After this, there could be no doubt of his attitude. In October, 1779, the New York Legislature passed an act of attainder against 58 persons "for adhering to the King." This

13

PLATE 9   LIVINGSTON HOUSE, DOBBS'S FERRY: PARLOUR

act adjudged their real and personal estates confiscate and declared that

> "each and every one of them who shall at any time hereafter be found in any part of this State shall be and are hereby adjudged and declared guilty of felony, and shall suffer Death."

Frederick Philipse, his sisters Susannah and Mary, and their husbands, Beverley Robinson and Roger Morris, fell under this savage ban. Thus by one act the Manor of Philipsborough was dissolved and the family's estates confiscated. In 1783, when the treaty of peace was signed and the British evacuated New York, Frederick Philipse, *"humiliated in spirit, blind of sight and broken in health,"* with his family and other Loyalists went to England. He died in 1786 and was buried in Chester Cathedral.

General Sir Henry Clinton made the Manor House his headquarters for a short time in 1779. When it was sold in 1785, under the act of attainder and confiscation, Cornelius P. Low bought it. From 1868 till 1908 it served first as the Village Hall, then the City Hall, of Yonkers. In 1908 the State acquired it and, in 1911, turned it over to the custody of the *American Scenic and Historic Preservation Society.*

When the first Frederick Philipse died, he left his son Adolphus all that vast tract known as the Upper Plantation. Adolphus made his home at CASTLE PHILIPSE (Plate 15) and the house became the centre of jurisdiction for the domain under his control. When Adolphus died in 1750, his nephew Frederick, second Lord, inherited the Upper Plantation; thus the whole of the original domain came again into the hands of a single proprietor and the Manor House at Yonkers was the seat of the entire jurisdiction. Castle Philipse, after its half-century or more of brilliant hospitality and domestic life, sank into a secondary position. During a long period it passed through so many vicissitudes and was so altered and spoiled by successive owners that at last it bore little

PLATE 10   LIVINGSTON HOUSE, DOBBS'S FERRY: DINING ROOM

semblance to the structure Frederick Philipse built in or about 1683.

It has now been taken over by John D. Rockefeller, jr., and is fortunately undergoing the same kind of painstaking, scholarly restoration that rehabilitated Williamsburg and made the ancient capital of Virginia a monument of unparallelled historical value. When the restoration is completed, Castle Philipse will once again disclose its 17th-century character and be a landmark worthy the history of the State.

At Dobbs's Ferry, the LIVINGSTON HOUSE (Plate 6), now the home of Mr. and Mrs. Messmore Kendall, like the Philipse Manor House, is also the result of several stages of growth. What is now the middle part of south or garden front indicates the extent of the old farmhouse, which belonged to the Manor of Philipsborough and, at the time of the Revolution, was occupied by Thomas Heyatt, a tenant of Frederick Philipse. When the Commis-

sioners of Forfeitures sold the confiscated Philipse estates, Philip Livingston, eldest son of Peter Van Brugh Livingston, bought the house and its farm of 233 acres on October 10, 1785. Philip Livingston was commonly known as "Gentleman Phil" because of his courtly manners, and the soubriquet serves to distinguish him from his uncle Philip the "Signer" and his cousin of the same name.

"Gentleman Phil" was graduated from King's (afterwards Columbia) College, studied law at the Temple in London and, after his return to America, was Registrar of the Prerogative Court of New York and Secretary to Governour Sir Henry Moore until the latter's death in 1769. Unlike his father, his uncle the "Signer" and most of his other Livingston relatives, "Gentleman Phil" was a Loyalist but, after the signing of peace, seems to have been leniently treated for, in 1788, he represented Westchester County in the New York Convention that ratified the Federal Constitution. It was during the Livingston ownership that the large western front of

PLATE 11   ODELL HOUSE, HARTSDALE: SOUTH FRONT   NO. 3 ON MAP

the house was added and other extensive improvements made to convert the erstwhile farmhouse into a handsome countryseat. In 1790 "Gentleman Phil" married Cornelia Van Horne of New York City. He occupied the house at Dobbs's Ferry until his death in 1810.

Local tradition has connected the house with several important events in Revolutionary history. Unfortunately documentary evidence to substantiate tradition is lacking.

Colonel JOHN ODELL's HOUSE (Plate 11), near Hartsdale, figured prominently for a little while during the Revolutionary War. In the summer of 1776, the newly-organised "Convention of Representatives of the State of New York" was a migratory body. On July 10th, just after tidings of the Declaration of Independence in Philadelphia, they had resolved to take steps to form a new State Government on the 16th but, when the day came, affairs had become too alarming for calm deliberation; they had to be content with passing only the most urgently needed enactments. Washington was about to abandon New York City, and British ships were anchored opposite Tarrytown. On the 27th the Convention removed to Harlem, thence to King's Bridge, and from King's Bridge to the Odell house, where they continued to sit until August 29th; then they rose again, to re-

sume sittings later at Fishkill. For a brief period, therefore, the house was the seat of State Government.

From July 6 to August 19, 1781, Comte de Rochambeau made the house his headquarters. It was the scene of not a little military gaiety and entertaining while the French and American armies lay encamped nearby. Albeit these parallel encampments lasted for a few weeks only, both commands took occasion to indulge in social diversions. Numerous banquets were given and frequently the tables were spread *"in the big barns adjoining the farmhouses where the generals had their headquarters."* The remains of bake ovens constructed by the French army cooks have been found nearby.

After the war, John Odell became Lieutenant-Colonel of a regiment of Westchester County Militia.

NEVIS (Plate 12), at Irvington, built in 1835, was the home of the Honourable James Alexander Hamilton, third son of Alexander Hamilton. Like his two elder brothers, Philip and Alexander, he was a graduate of Columbia College, completing his course there in 1805. He was a major in the War of 1812 and inspector in the United States Army. Under President Jackson he served for a time as Acting Secretary of State until the appointment of

PLATE 12

NEVIS, IRVINGTON: WEST OR RIVER FRONT

PLATE 13   NEVIS, IRVINGTON: EAST FRONT

PLATE 14   SUNNYSIDE, TARRYTOWN: WEST FRONT   NO. 5 ON MAP

Castle Philipse, Tarrytown: View from South

Plate 15

19

PLATE 16   SLEEPY HOLLOW CHURCH, TARRYTOWN: APSE AND NORTH SIDE   NO. 7 ON MAP

PLATE 17   VAN CORTLANDT MANOR HOUSE, CROTON-ON-HUDSON: ENTRANCE   NO. 8 ON MAP

Martin Van Buren to that office in 1829. The same year he was appointed United States District Attorney for the Southern District of New York and had a *"long and eventful life in the law, politics and literature."* His *Reminiscences*, published in 1869, contain a wealth of invaluable contemporary historical material. He died at Nevis (named for the island of his father's birth) in 1878 at the age of ninety. Nevis now, very appropriately, belongs to Columbia University.

SUNNYSIDE (Plate 14), Washington Irving's home at Tarrytown, started with Wolfert Acker's little old Dutch farmhouse that Irving bought in 1835. By subsequent additions the house has grown to such an extent that the original structure is now only an inconspicuous portion of the whole. It was the little old farmhouse, however, that fired Irving's imagination and inspired so many of the tales that have delighted his own and succeeding generations. Irving's affection for Sunnyside and the story of his life there are too well known to need extended comment. As a literary shrine, Sunnyside holds a position analogous to that of Abbotsford in Scotland.

The VAN CORTLANDT MANOR HOUSE (Plate 18) on the Albany Post Road still presents its ancient unspoiled aspect to northbound travellers crossing the long bridge at the mouth of the Croton River.

In 1638 Oloff Stevense Van Cortlandt left his home in Holland and accompanied Director-General Kieft to New Amsterdam. Not long afterwards he married Annetje Loockermans who, with her brother Gouvert, had come to look after considerable investments they had ventured in the Dutch Colony. Their eldest child, Stephanus, born in 1643, later became first Lord of the Manor of Cortlandt. Entering early into the public life of the city, his first appointment was to the Court of Assises. When only thirty-four, he was elected Mayor, the first native-born American to fill that post in New York. In 1693 he was commissioned Colonel, commanding the King's County Militia. Governour Sir Edmund Andros appointed him first Judge in Admiralty and likewise an Associate Judge of the Colonial Court. In rapid succession he became Chancellor, Collector of Revenues, last of all, Chief-Justice of the Supreme Court. Apart from public duties, he pursued an active mercantile career and also found opportunity to serve Church interests as Senior Warden of Trinity Parish.

In 1677 Stephanus got license from Governour Andros to buy lands from the Indians and for a number of years increased his holdings, especially in Westchester County, until he owned the east bank of the Hudson from the mouth of the Croton River to a point north of Anthony's Nose. This tract extended eastward to the Connecticut boundary with an area of about 87,000 acres. When he had completed the continuity of his river boundary by a purchase from Governour Dongan, he applied for a Royal Charter confirming his title. This charter, creating the Manor of Cortlandt, was granted June 17, 1697.

Unlike most of the other Hudson Valley manors, the Manor of Cortlandt kept its original Manor House throughout its history. It is known to have been standing in 1681 but, in all likelihood, was built considerably earlier—perhaps as early as 1665. Erected originally for a fort, its thick stone walls pierced with loopholes (all of which remain to-day), it had at first a flat stone roof like the Mohawk Valley forts built about 1640. It was at first a refuge for settlers in the neighbourhood whenever the Indians became dangerously excited at their tribal feasts and dances. Later, Governour Dongan seems to have used it as a hunting lodge, for occasional holidays. When all danger from Indians was past, the stone roof gave place to an upper storey with dormers.

Within, the hall runs through to the back of the house. There, the panelling, hopelessly damaged or torn away during the Revolution, was replaced. Elsewhere, the original 17th-century panelling remains. To the right, on entering, is the parlour, panelled on one side. Within the fireplace, and projecting somewhat beyond the surrounding woodwork, is a small iron hood—put there to improve the draught—which may have inspired Benjamin Franklin with the idea for the famous Franklin Stove. Certain it is that the great philosopher, once when he spent a night at the Manor House, slept in this room, then a bedchamber; the parlour was then on the lower floor. Franklin enquired about and commented on this hood; the Franklin Stove appeared soon afterwards. The natural presumption is that the Manor House fireplace planted the seed of an invention.

At the left, on entering, is the dining-room. Opposite the fireplace hangs a portrait of the Indian chief Joseph Brant, above it his scarf, which he gave as a token of friendship to an ancestor of the family. Brant dined at the table in this room and, at one time or another, every Colonial governour, as well as nearly every person else of consequence in the Colonies, dined at it also. Quite apart from historic associations, it is an exceptional piece of furniture. It is of gate pattern and the top is a perfect oval of mahogany. Oloff Van Cortlandt brought it with him from Holland in 1638, along with several other treasured family possessions.

Philip Van Cortlandt, the son of Stephanus and Gertrude Schuyler, his wife, became the second Lord of the Manor at the death of his father in 1700. He married Catharine, daughter of Abraham de Peyster,

PLATE 18   VAN CORTLANDT MANOR HOUSE, CROTON-ON-HUDSON: SOUTH FRONT

PLATE 19   VAN CORTLANDT MANOR HOUSE, CROTON-ON-HUDSON:
                              EAST END, FROM GARDEN

PLATE 20   VAN CORTLANDT MANOR HOUSE, CROTON-ON-HUDSON: NORTH FRONT

PLATE 21   VAN CORTLANDT MANOR HOUSE, CROTON-ON-HUDSON: STAIR

whose house at Beacon appears on page 49. Great landowner and merchant, Philip also took an active part in public affairs. Appointed to the Provincial Council in 1729, he was also a Commissioner of Indian Affairs and took part in settling the boundary disputes with Connecticut. Dying in 1747, Pierre, his fifth and youngest son (born 1721), succeeded him as third Lord of the Manor.

Pierre Van Cortlandt and his wife, Joanna Livingston, gave up New York City as a place of partial residence and, in 1749, came to make their home at the Manor House the year round. Besides the numerous relatives and friends who always found a warm welcome at the Manor House, there came now also nearly everyone who bore an active or important part in the affairs of the Province or country, for Pierre Van Cortlandt played a conspicuous rôle. From 1768 to 1775 he sat in the Provincial Assembly for the Manor of Cortlandt. As the struggle with the Mother Country became imminent, his sympathies were strongly on the side of the Colonies. When Governour Tryon came to the Manor House and told his host

"the great favours that would be granted him if he would espouse the royal cause and adhere to King and Parliament, Van Cortlandt answered him that he was chosen a representative by unanimous approbation of a people who placed confidence in his integrity to use all his ability for their benefit and good of his country."

This course he was determined to pursue. In November 1775 he was chosen deputy to the Second Provincial Congress, and sat in the third and fourth congresses till May, 1777, when he was elected President of the Council of Safety. In 1777 he became Lieutenant-Governour of the State, discharging the duties of both Governour and Lieutenant-Governour during the Revolutionary War, since General George Clinton, the Governour, was busied with his military duties. The office of Lieutenant-Governour he held until 1795; in 1788 he was likewise President of the State Convention that ratified the Federal Constitution.

When they came within the neighbourhood, the American officers, and the foreign officers who served with the Continental Army, paid their respects at the Manor House. Hither came the Comte de Rochambeau, the Marquis de la Fayette, the Duc de Lauzun and many more of equal fame, while the name of Baron von Steuben stands forth in a long list of eminent foreign personages because of his huge enjoyment of roasted oysters in the Manor House kitchen, a form of gastronomic frolic in which he had never before indulged. General Washington and his aides many times enjoyed the Manor House hospitality.

Only once in its history was the house left desolate. In 1777, when the men of the family were con-

stantly away in the service of their country, the unsettled conditions of the neighbourhood made it no longer safe for the mother and her children to remain there; with flocks, herds and household gear they removed to a farm near Rhinebeck. Only a few slaves were left in charge, and they lived in constant dread. Once, when they were crouched in their hiding place under the roof, they heard a band of raiders, seated on the verandah, making plans to burn the house. Fortunately, the advance of Generals Greene and Knox at this point sent them flying and saved the house. More than three years elapsed before it was safe to return. Much wanton damage had been done in the meanwhile, but the destruction had been repaired and the house had assumed its wonted appearance when, in July 1781, Washington stopped on his way to Peekskill after he had *crossed the new bridge over the Croton,"* and Baron de Kalb, General Philip Schuyler and many others paid visits. In 1783, when Washington made his triumphal entry into New York City after the British evacuation, Pierre Van Cortlandt accompanied him and left an account of the progress in his diary.

In 1814 Pierre Van Cortlandt died at the age of ninety-four and his eldest son, General Philip Van Cortlandt, succeeded him as head of the family. The close friend of Washington, Rochambeau and la Fayette, General Van Cortlandt was one of the founders of the Society of the Cincinnati. When the Marquis de la Fayette made his tour through the United States in 1824, General Van Cortlandt was of his party. For sixteen years he sat in the United States Congress and in other ways also rendered valuable public services to his State and country as long as he lived. At his death, in 1831, his brother General Pierre Van Cortlandt succeeded to the possession of the Manor House. Descendants of Oloff Van Cortlandt still live there.

The VAN CORTLANDT HOUSE (Plate 25) just north of Peekskill, used by Pierre the third Lord of the Manor when it was more convenient for him to be there than at the Manor House, is a Georgian dwelling of ample dimensions. Sold out of the family about the middle of the 19th century, its later owners succumbed to the then prevalent craze for gables, fretted bargeboards and jigsaw decoration. During part of the Revolutionary War, Cornelia Beekman, Pierre Van Cortlandt's daughter and a person of courage and determination, occupied the house. Though her home was frequently within the danger zone, she remained there undaunted. Once, indeed, she took refuge some miles back in the country but stayed away only a day and night. When she came back, raiders had left not a stick of furniture save one bedstead, and of provisions naught but one ham.

PLATE 22   VAN CORTLANDT MANOR HOUSE, CROTON-ON-HUDSON:
THE "PROPHETS' CHAMBER"

PLATE 23   VAN CORTLANDT MANOR HOUSE, CROTON-ON-HUDSON: PARLOUR

General Patterson was at one time quartered in her house; Washington visited her frequently when he was in the neighbourhood. When Washington made the house his headquarters, tradition says that the scarcity of furniture, owing to the recency of the raid just mentioned, obliged his aides to improvise bedsteads by placing chairs together.

Cornelia Beekman unconsciously played a part in the capture of Major André. Lieutenant Jack Webb, acting aide to General Washington, came to the house and left with Mrs. Beekman for safe keeping a bag containing a new uniform and some gold, asking her to send it to him at *"brother Sam's"* when he sent word. About a fortnight later, Joshua Hett Smith appeared and asked for the bag, saying Jack

Webb was in Peekskill and had asked him to get it. Mrs. Beekman was on the point of handing over the bag, but suddenly thought better of it and refused. Smith was insistent and urged that as Mrs. Beekman knew him well it must be all right to let him have the uniform. Mrs. Beekman answered that she knew Smith so well she didn't trust him. There was nothing for him to do but go away disappointed. This was just at the time Smith was trying to get André back within the British lines. Somehow he had learned the whereabouts of Webb's new uniform and hoped to get it for André, knowing André and Webb were about of a size. Had Smith succeeded in getting it, André, in all likelihood, would never have been captured.

PLATE 24   VAN CORTLANDT MANOR HOUSE, CROTON-ON-HUDSON: DINING ROOM

PLATE 25   VAN CORTLANDT HOUSE, PEEKSKILL: SOUTH FRONT   NO. 10 ON MAP

PUTNAM COUNTY

BOSCOBEL (Plate 27), known also as the Dyck-man-Cruger House, was rescued from destruction, moved from Cruger Park to a new site at Garrison-on-Hudson, and reopened as Boscobel Restoration in May, 1961. It was built by States Morris Dyckman in 1804, completed only after his death in 1806. A member of the Dyckman family of the Bronx, States was an American farm boy who traveled widely and lived in England for many years. He was a person of self-acquired learning and elegance who intended in Boscobel to re-create some of the finest qualities of outstanding English homes of the 18th century. States' friends in England included William Adam, nephew of the great architect Robert Adam, whose influence is apparent in Boscobel's design. After States' death the house was lived in by his widow, Elizabeth and their only son, Peter Corne Dyckman. When Peter's daughter, Eliza Letitia Dyckman married John Peach Cruger, the house became identified with the Cruger family as well.

Boscobel passed out of the Cruger family and was thrice threatened with destruction. Sold to a house-wrecker for $35, it was saved from demolition by private citizens who lived in the Hudson Valley area. Private funds, including a one million dollar grant from The Reader's Digest Foundation, have since insured its perpetuation. Furnishings and accessories for Boscobel were assembled in Europe and America and represent States Dyckman's taste and his plans for furnishing his home. Several pieces acquired by the Restoration were in the original house.

Boscobel now fronts on a 36-acre plot some 200 feet above the Hudson facing West Point. Its stately interior matches and perhaps even exceeds the exterior in the beauty and delicacy of its various features and details. From the front door one enters a great hall crossed by a triple arcade and graced by a Moorefield carpet personally designed by Robert Adam. Beyond this a broad stair branches in two flights at the landing, where the setting is capped by a magnificent Palladian window. The double staircases then ascend to a large library and to Boscobel's four bedrooms and nursery. Throughout the house, mantels, doorways, plasterwork and other details reflect the refinement and elegance of the Federal Era. A carriage house placed on the property adds to the historic and aesthetic values of the rescued mansion.

PLATE 26   STRANG-DURRIN HOUSE, PEEKSKILL: SOUTH FRONT   No. 11 on Map
              AN UNSPOILED EXAMPLE OF AN 18TH CENTURY FARMHOUSE

PLATE 27   BOSCOBEL RESTORATION, GARRISON-ON-HUDSON,   NO. 9 ON MAP
                        SOUTH FRONT FACING RIVER.
              INSET: PORTRAIT OF STATES MORRIS DYCKMAN, BUILDER.

PLATE 28   BOSCOBEL RESTORATION, GARRISON-ON-HUDSON:
                    MAIN STAIR HALL, LOOKING TO RIVER.

COLONEL BEVERLEY ROBINSON built BEVERLY (Plate 29) in 1758, at the foot of Sugar Loaf Mountain, in Philipstown in the Highlands. He described his dwelling as *"a wooden house lined with brick . . . added to afterwards."* Architecturally unpretentious, but roomy and comfortable, it did not lack becoming elegance inside; a number of the rooms were panelled and the appointments in keeping with the quality and means of the occupants, who maintained an unostentatious but lavish hospitality. The panelled dining-room, scene of Arnold's ill-fated breakfast party, was in the middle part. This, along with the higher eastern part of the building, formed the master's quarters; the low western end contained kitchen and service arrangements.

Beverley Robinson, born in Virginia in 1722, was a friend of George Washington; their friendship endured till the firm convictions of each drew them to opposite sides in the Revolutionary War. On the strength of old friendship it was that Robinson appealed to Washington on behalf of André. Robinson early entered military life when, in 1746,

"he raised a company in the service of the King and Government of Great Britain in an expedition against Canada, and was ordered with his Company to the Colony of New York; in the fortress of the said Colony he did duty (the greatest part of the time) until the conclusion of that war, when the forces raised for the expedition were disbanded."

Attracted by prospects the growing city of New York offered enterprising men, Robinson determined to settle there. He associated himself in business with Oliver De Lancey, who afterwards commanded a Loyalist brigade in the Revolution. The firm of De Lancey, Robinson & Co. once occupied what was later Fraunces's Tavern, *"being the corner house next to the Royal Exchange."*

In 1748 Colonel Robinson married Susannah Philipse, eldest sister of Frederick, third and last Lord of the Manor of Philipsborough. For some years following their marriage they lived in the city; with them Mary Philipse, who later married Roger Morris, spent much time. It was during one of her city sojourns that George Washington is said first to have met and fallen in love with Mary, to whom also he is said to have offered his heart and hand, only to learn that Roger Morris had been before him and won the prize.

When they had built Beverly, Colonel and Mrs. Robinson went to live permanently in what was then part of Dutchess County. The estate embraced some 60,000 acres, Mrs. Robinson's share of the Philipse lands. The Colonel was a practical farmer on a large scale. There were over 1500 acres in the home farm alone, besides mills and other features that required constant supervision. In 1785, when he preferred compensation claims for part of his losses due to adherence to the Crown, Captain Duncan Campbell testified before the Royal Commissioners that

"Mr. Robinson was not only beloved and respected by his tenants, but was also universally respected and esteemed by all in the County in which he lived."

Always a loyal Church of England supporter, he was really the founder of St. Philip's Chapel in the Highlands, for which he gave the land, and also enough besides for a glebe. Of the united parish of St. Peter's (Peekskill) and St. Philip's he was the first church-warden and to his generosity were due many benefactions the fruit of which the parish continues to enjoy. It was doubtless due to Robinson's support of St. Philip's Chapel that it was later called a "Tory Church." The story goes that once during the Revolutionary War, when General Washington was riding past St. Philip's with one of his staff-officers, the officer, pointing with his crop, said, *"That is a Tory church, Sir."* To which Washington, who was a vestryman in his own Virginia parish, replied, *"It is my church."*

Although the Whigs were anxious to secure Robinson's interest on the American side, he supported the King's cause from the first, both from conviction and sense of loyalty. For a time, local consideration saved him some of the annoyances other Loyalists suffered but, in February, 1777, the Dutchess County Commissioners required from him an oath of allegiance to the American cause. That, he declared, *'he would never take.'* Unequivocally taking his stand, he raised a regiment for the King. Many of the recruits were his own tenants; nearly all were from his own county. This fact is an index to the strength of Loyalist sentiment in the Province, not only amongst families of wealth and rank, but also amongst those of the plainer sort.

Under the circumstances, it was impossible to avert confiscation of the family estate. Immediately on his departure from Beverly, Robinson's *"personal property was seized by the Commissioners of Sequestration and ordered for instant sale."* Samuel Verplanck appealed to James Duane to stay the proceedings, but in vain. The Commissioners sold household furniture, live stock, slaves, farming implements and growing crops. Turned out of house and home, Mrs. Robinson and her children had to seek shelter in New York along with other Loyalist refugees. Colonel Robinson fought with distinction throughout the war. When the British Army evacuated New York City in 1783, the Robinsons re-

(Courtesy of William Beverley Rogers, Esq.)

No. 12 on Map

BEVERLY, GARRISON-ON-HUDSON: SOUTH FRONT
(HOUSE DESTROYED BY FIRE, 1892)

PLATE 29

35

moved to England. After the delays in adjusting such matters, Colonel Robinson got partial compensation for the loss of his estates in America so that he could live in comfortable retirement in his advancing years. He died at Bath. Descendants of Beverley Robinson and Susannah Philipse are now living in both England and America.

Close following seizure of the Robinsons' estate begins the dramatic chapter in Beverly's story. There Generals Putnam and Parsons made their headquarters on several occasions in 1778 and 1779; in 1780, when General Arnold was given command of West Point, he chose to make his residence there. Mrs. Arnold was with him. Arnold used the old house on Constitution Island as his office; between Beverly, his office and West Point he travelled in his barge. On the fateful morning of September 25, 1780, Washington and la Fayette were expected for breakfast at Beverly. They were returning from Hartford before the time originally set, and had sent word they would start early from Fishkill (18 miles distant) and breakfast with Arnold. When they came opposite West Point, Washington turned his horse towards the river. La Fayette, riding beside him, said,

"General, you're going in the wrong direction; you know Mrs. Arnold's waiting breakfast for us, and that road will take us out of the way." Washington answered good-naturedly, "O, I know you young men are all in love with Mrs. Arnold, and wish to get where she is as soon as possible. You can go and take your breakfast with her, and tell her not to wait for me; I must ride down and examine the redoubts on this side of the river, and shall be there in a short time."

The officers, however, stayed with Washington, except two aides whom he sent to tell Mrs. Arnold to go on with breakfast.

Breakfast was waiting when the aides reached Beverly; they sat down with the General and Mrs. Arnold. Arnold was silent and moody. The British forces had not appeared to attack West Point, as previously planned. Washington had come back two full days before he was expected. Something must have gone agley. While they were at breakfast came a letter from Colonel Jameson. Instead of welcome news, the letter said André was a prisoner in Jameson's custody. Arnold controlled himself, made his excuses to his guests, and asked them to tell General Washington that an unexpected message had called him immediately to West Point but that he would soon be back. He ordered his horse, then went up to Mrs. Arnold's room and sent for her. When she came, he told her quickly what had happened, bade her good-bye and leaving her in a swoon, rushed downstairs, flung himself into the saddle and made off toward the dock by a precipitous short-cut—ever since known as Arnold's Path—whither he had hastily summoned his rowers. Driving them into the barge when they were but half ready, with mingled threats and promises he urged them down the river at top speed. As they passed Verplanck's Point his white handkerchief answered for a signal to Colonel Livingston, in command there, and also to Captain Sutherland of the *Vulture* lying at anchor a few miles downstream. Coming alongside, he was taken aboard and was safe from the consequences of his misdoing. He then despatched a letter to General Washington, apprising him of his defection, and enclosed another for Mrs. Arnold.

When Washington reached Beverly, he was surprised not to find Arnold. Learning he had been hastily summoned to West Point, Washington set out thither expecting to find him. At West Point there was no salute. This amazed and nettled Washington; he was always a stickler for proprieties, whether in military or civil life. As he started up from the dock, he met Colonel Lamb coming down. The Colonel apologised for the apparent neglect of courtesy, explaining he knew nothing of Washington's intended visit. *"Sir, is not General Arnold here?"* said Washington. *"No, Sir,"* said Colonel Lamb, *"he's not been here these two days, nor have I heard from him within that time."* Washington's suspicions were aroused; he was puzzled. Nevertheless, he inspected all the works, and about noon recrossed the river to Beverly. On the way from the dock to the house Colonel Alexander Hamilton met him and told him what had happened. Colonel Jameson's messenger—despatched to Hartford with papers taken from André and bearing André's letter to Arnold—hearing at Danbury of Washington's return by the upper road, had ridden post haste and reached Beverly four hours after Arnold's flight. Washington was at West Point and the messenger had given Hamilton the papers. Straightway Washington sent Hamilton to Verplanck's Point to tell Colonel Livingston to intercept Arnold. But Arnold had already been safe aboard the *Vulture* for several hours, and as Hamilton reached Verplanck's Point a messenger from the *Vulture* was approaching with a flag of truce. He brought Arnold's letter to Washington which, besides announcing his act, besought protection for Mrs. Arnold and his child. This letter, and the letter to Mrs. Arnold, Hamilton immediately forwarded to Washington at Beverly, then hastened to execute the rest of Washington's instructions. Major André was taken to Beverly on the morning of the 26th, then sent across to West Point the evening of the same day.

After this short but intensely dramatic episode, Beverly relapsed into its wonted quietude. The house was destroyed by fire in 1892. Its site will always hold haunting memories of André's pathetic figure and Arnold's black treachery.

PLATE 31   MANDEVILLE HOUSE, GARRISON-ON-HUDSON: SOUTH FRONT

PLATE 32   MANDEVILLE HOUSE, GARRISON-ON-HUDSON: NORTH FRONT

PLATE 33   MANDEVILLE HOUSE, GARRISON-ON-HUDSON: HALL

The story of WOOD CRAG (Plate 38), the old house on Constitution Island (or Martelaer's Rock) dovetails into the stories of Beverly and West Point. The rocky islet on which the house stands was originally included in the possessions of the Philipse family. "Martelaer's Rock" is a corruption of the Dutch *Martelaer's Rach,* meaning "Martyr's Reach," a name apparently given in allusion to the struggle against wind and tide often required on this "reach" of the river to weather this rocky point. The name "Constitution Island" comes from Fort Constitution, established there at the time of the Revolution. The name of the fort must have been given with reference to the *British* Constitution; the fort was built (1775) before the Declaration of Independence and before the State of New York or the United States had assumed corporate existence, much less adopted constitutions.

At the beginning of the war it was evident that the strategic point of control of the whole upper river was here—hence the anxiety to fortify it thoroughly. The original plan of defense did not include works at West Point, but it was soon plain that hostile artillery on the high promontory overlooking Constitution Island could immediately render the island fort untenable.

> "Because of its geographical situation with respect to the already garrisoned defenses on the east bank of the river, the site of the new defenses derived its present name—West Point."

Thus Constitution Island was the parent of West Point.

In 1836, Henry W. Warner, of New York City, bought Constitution Island and built the house, which he called Wood Crag—now one of the chief objects of care to the Martelaer's Rock Association—incorporating the smaller house already standing there before the Revolution. In this older house where Arnold had his office, he is said to have written his letter about the removal of a link from the chain that held the log boom stretched across the river at this, its narrowest, point, in order to ob-

PLATE 34   MANDEVILLE HOUSE, GARRISON-ON-HUDSON: PARLOUR

struct the passage of British war ships should they attempt to ascend the Hudson. Arnold's ostensible reason for removing the link was to repair the chain; his real reason was to assist the British ships at his proposed surrender of West Point.

As the home for many years of the Warner sisters, Wood Crag became a literary shrine. Here, in 1850, Miss Susan Warner wrote *The Wide, Wide World,* a book that left an indelible impress on an older generation. Miss Warner also wrote *Diana* and *My Desire,* as well as some thirty-odd other books, nearly all of which enjoyed wide popularity in their day. Miss Anna Warner's long life was given to useful works and she gave much of her time to conducting a Bible class for the students at West Point and other ministrations to the cadets, who long afterwards revered her memory. Through the generosity of Miss Warner and Mrs. Russell Sage, Constitution Island was given to the United States in September, 1908, and by the Government accepted as *"an addition to the Military Reservation of West Point and*

to be for the use of the United States Military Academy."

Washington was first officially mentioned by the Continental Congress in connection with the defenses on Constitution Island; the breastworks commenced there in 1775, by order of the Continental Congress, were later completed under the supervision of Kosciusko; and there, on December 20, 1783, Washington's body guard were mustered out.

The MANDEVILLE HOUSE (Plate 30), at Garrison-on-Hudson, built about 1735, was one of the three best houses in the neighbourhood in the Revolutionary era—the others were Beverly and a house at West Point. In 1770, when St. Peter's Parish was established in Peekskill, with the Chapel of St. Philip in the Highlands, it was arranged that the parson should hold at least two services a month at Mr. Mandeville's house. The first services were held there late in 1770 and were continued regularly until the nearby St. Philip's Chapel was finished in

PLATE 35   MANDEVILLE HOUSE, GARRISON-ON-HUDSON: DINING ROOM

1771 or 1772. In 1920, at the 150th anniversary of the parish, a service was again held in the house.

Jacob Mandeville—grandson of Yellis Jansen Mandeville, who came from Holland to New Amsterdam in the *Gude Vrouw* in 1659—was born in New York City about 1709. In 1735 he married Sarah Davenport, daughter of Thomas Davenport of Cold Spring. It was about that time that he leased 400 acres in the Philipse Patent for £5 yearly, and built his house. The original part of the house was what is now the dining-room and the room behind it, with an open attic above. A kitchen wing was the first addition and later, but well before the Revolution, came the present parlour and the bedroom above it. The library was not built till after 1850.

On the direct road from Westchester County and the southwestern parts of Connecticut to West Point, officers of high rank frequently came to the house during the Revolution. General Putnam made it his headquarters from May 25, 1777, until late in October, and there Mrs. Putnam died soon after the fall of Forts Clinton and Montgomery. In Washington's *Headquarters-Expense Account* there is an entry of July 26, 1779, *"to cash paid at Mandeville's for house rooms etc., £ 2:5:0."*; apparently the Commander-in-Chief stayed there on one of his journeys. Writing from West Point to General du Portail and Colonel Alexander Hamilton, Washington mentions a letter from General Heath dated *"Mandeville's October 21, 1779, 4:00 o'clock P.M.,"* and later, in writing General Heath, he speaks of *"your old quarters at Mandeville's."* In November, 1781, it seems likely that General Howe had quarters there. In the library at West Point is a letter mentioning that *"some of the younger officers were going over to Mandeville's to see the girls."*

Jacob Mandeville died in 1784. The next year, when the Commissioners sold the sequestered Philipse lands, Mandeville's son-in-law, Joshua Nelson, who was still living there, bought the farm. The house and part of the farm remained in his family until sold to a Mrs. Brown in the 1840's. Richard

PLATE 36   MANDEVILLE HOUSE, GARRISON-ON-HUDSON:
        DINING ROOM FIREPLACE AND PANELLING

PLATE 37   MANDEVILLE HOUSE, GARRISON-ON-HUDSON: KITCHEN

Upjohn, the architect, bought the place in 1852 and remodelled the house in the taste of the time. Colonel Julian A. Benjamin, the present owner, with the constant advice and aid of Miss Nancy Allan, has completely restored the house and furnished it with contemporary appointments.

Lying just to the east of the Albany Post Road, at Indian Brook between Garrison-on-Hudson and Cold Spring, THE BIRD AND BOTTLE (Plate 39) began life about 1761—perhaps a few years earlier—as Warren's Tavern. When the Post Road was little more than a horse trail, John Warren's tavern was a welcome sight to weary travellers of pre-Revolutionary days. As travel increased on this first highway through Putnam (then Dutchess) County—it had been much improved since its horse trail beginnings —Warren's Tavern became a famous stopping place. Somewhat later, stagecoaches between Albany and New York regularly changed horses there, while passengers and driver often stayed the night. In

1776 the inn passed to Absalom Nelson, at his marriage to Esther Warren, and thenceforth was known as Nelson's Tavern. Its success continued under Absalom Nelson, and during the post-Revolutionary period it attained its greatest renown. The building of the Highland Turnpike (now the Albany Post Road—U. S. Route 9), which ran parallel to the old Post Road and ended at Nelson's Tavern, greatly increased highway traffic between New York and Albany, and Nelson's Tavern became one of the best known and esteemed ordinaries in that part of the State.

With the increase of boat travel on the Hudson and, finally, the coming of the railroad, life at Nelson's Tavern gradually waned. At last, custom had so dwindled that the inn ceased to be a place of public entertainment and for a long time was a private dwelling. It so continued until 1939, when George W. Perkins, of Cold Spring, wishing to preserve for Putnam County one of its historic buildings, bought it with intent to restore it and have it

PLATE 39   THE BIRD AND BOTTLE, GARRISON-ON-HUDSON: SOUTH FRONT   NO. 15 ON MAP

PLATE 40   THE BIRD AND BOTTLE, GARRISON-ON-HUDSON: TAP ROOM FIREPLACE

again conducted as an ordinary, and in a manner worthy of its traditions. Completely restored and equipped under the supervision of Mr. and Mrs. Charles Burnham Stearns, The Bird and Bottle is conducted by them as an hostelry successfully combining modern comfort and convenience with the essential spirit and characteristics of the 18th century coaching-inn.

DUTCHESS COUNTY

THE TELLER HOMESTEAD (Plate 42) at Beacon is a symbol of the whole neighbourhood's history. In 1654, Francis Rombout, a Huguenot born at Hesselt in Flanders, sailed as supercargo on a ship bound for New Netherland. A mere lad at the time, after faithfully discharging his duties, he had to sue the captain for his wages. That he did so was indicative of his character—his energy, determination and love of justice. As a New York merchant he prospered, bought a valuable property on Broadway and built himself a substantial stone house, surrounded by an orchard and garden. He was evidently a man of taste, as well as an energetic merchant and man of affairs, for he is said to have imported for his own satisfaction the first table linen used in America.

Besides diligently managing his mercantile interests, he was an active member and elder in the Dutch Reformed Church, and found time to serve the city in sundry public offices—as Schepen under Dutch rule, and afterwards under English rule as Alderman. At the Dutch recapture of New York he was continued in office and, in 1679, after the restoration of English control, he was Mayor, succeeding Stephanus Van Cortlandt in that post.

In 1682 Francis Rombout and Gulian Verplanck jointly filed a petition for a land grant and permission to buy from the Indians a fertile tract on the east bank of the Hudson extending from Fishkill almost to Poughkeepsie, later known as the Rombout Patent or Precinct. The same year Governour Dongan licensed this purchase, which was peaceably and honestly carried out. They say that Rombout bargained with the Indians for *"all the land he could see"*; he thereupon climbed to the top of Mount Beacon to extend his outlook. Tradition also says that during the bargaining the future Patentees sat at one side of a table while the Wappinger chiefs sat opposite. A round sum of Royals—a Royal equalled a half-sovereign—was laid on the board as the purchase price. This the Indians repeatedly pushed back, saying *"More, More!"* until the bargain satisfied them. The deed of sale, dated 1683, was then duly drawn, witnessed and executed. In 1685, soon after the accession of King James II, came the confirmation or "exemplification" of the grant. Prior to this, Gulian Verplanck had died and his widow had married Jacobus Kip, now substituted as representative for the interests of Verplanck's children. Stephanus Van Cortlandt had also been admitted to a third share in the purchase, so the exemplification was issued in the names of Rombout, Kip and Van Cortlandt.

By his third wife, Helena Teller Van Ball—daughter of William Teller, one of the Patentees of

Schenectady—Francis Rombout had a daughter Catheryna, born in 1687. To her he willed his house in Broadway and *"his land in the Wappins"*—his third share in the Rombout Patent. Catheryna, destined to become famous as a colonial dame of pre-eminent character and pioneer achievement, in November 1703 married Roger Brett, of Somersetshire, a young Lieutenant in the British Navy who had accompanied his friend Lord Cornbury, when Queen Anne sent out that eccentric cousin of hers to govern the Province of New York. Determined to live in the country and develop her land in the Rombout Patent, Madame Brett and her husband, in the summer of 1708, mortgaged their city house *"for 240 pounds current money."* In 1707 the Rombout Patent had been partitioned into *"three long, narrow parcels, each containing a stretch of river front, and water privileges by adjointure to the two creeks, the Fish Kill and Wappingers."* Lot Number One, in the drawing, fell to Madame Brett, while the Verplanck heirs got Lot Number Two, just to the north of them, on the river and on Wappingers Creek *"in the middle"*; the third or northernmost Lot, on the river and the upper part of Wappingers Creek, went to the Van Cortlandts.

By this division the Bretts possessed the fertile valley of the Fish Kill, a broad stretch along the river, and *"the north side of Wappingers Creek from its mouth to beyond the present site of Wappingers Falls."* On the banks of the Fish Kill, which gave them a valuable water power, they built a mill and a dwelling, presumably with the proceeds of the mortgage on the town house. The following year, 1709, *"Roger Brett of the Fishkills in the County of Dutchess, Gentleman, and Catheryna, his wife,"* sold to William Peartrie the mill, dwelling and 300 acres of land adjoining. It was in 1709, upon selling the mill and mill house, that the Bretts built the house now called Locust Grove or the Teller House. After selling the mill and mill house, Madame Brett exercised a woman's privilege of changing her mind; the next year she bought them back along with the land pertaining to them. From then until 1743, when she sold the mill property to her kinsman, Abraham de Peyster, she managed the enterprise with energy and success. For many years the people of Dutchess and Orange Counties depended largely *"upon this mill for their daily bread."* At one time all roads thereabouts seemed to lead *"to Madame Brett's Mill,"* and it was customary to quote distances and directions *"From Hackensack to Madame Brett's Mill,"* *"From Wiccopee to Madame Brett's Mill,"* and so on.

The Bretts had three sons, Francis, Robert and Rivery, the last so named because he was born on

PLATE 41   ABRAHAM DE PEYSTER HOUSE, BEACON: SOUTH FRONT   No. 16 on Map

PLATE 42   LOCUST GROVE (TELLER HOMESTEAD), BEACON: EAST FRONT   NO. 17 ON MAP

the Hudson River when his parents were coming home from New York in their sloop. In 1726 Lieutenant Brett met a tragic death; returning from New York, the boom of his boat knocked him overboard just as he was entering the mouth of the Fish Kill. Thence onward, all the burden of developing and administering a large estate fell on the shoulders of Madame Brett, aided only by her sons. She was fully equal to the task, however. In addition to her other sterling qualities, she was clear-headed and possessed business acumen and indomitable energy. She is said to have ridden daily on horseback over her lands, directing her slaves and superintending her varied affairs. A woman of peculiarly dynamic character, she was a power in the development of the whole region and left the impress of her personality in many quarters. Activity and locomotion seemed inseparable from the story of her life. She not only journeyed back and forth to New York by sloop and made the daily rounds of her farm in the saddle but, in 1710, when the first place of worship was

established in the neighbourhood—the Lutheran church of the German Palatines at Newburgh—she was accustomed to canoe across the river on Sundays to attend service. Sometimes she made her progresses in a manner fully befitting a lady of quality. In his *Local Tales and Sketches*, H. D. B. Bailey describes her arrival at the wedding of the Dutch pastor who served the two congregations of Fishkill and Poughkeepsie:

"As the hour of twelve drew near, the excitement became intense and what added to the enthusiasm was the appearance of Madame Brett, in her coach drawn by four horses, coming down Main Street [Poughkeepsie] with two negroes on the front and one on the rear of the coach, whose business was to open the door."

Prior to her death, in 1764, she devised her property to her son Francis, and the children of her son Robert, predeceased—Rivery had died in early life—and in that part of her will touching her slaves she directed that if they were sold, certain of them should have the right to choose their own masters.

No. 18 on Map

Mount Gulian, Beacon: West or River Front
(House destroyed by fire, 1931)

Plate 43

PLATE 44   CHRYSTIE HOUSE, BEACON: SOUTH FRONT   NO. 19 ON MAP

PLATE 45   CHRYSTIE HOUSE, BEACON: PARLOUR

Francis Brett and his wife, Catharine Margaret Van Wyck, with their eight children continued to occupy the house and, in due time, their daughter Hannah married Henry Schenck, who became a major in the Continental Army. While he was Quartermaster, the ample cellar of the house was stored with rations for the soldiers, and once a detachment of exhausted men was ranged in rows on the floor of the east room to sleep off their fatigue. In 1791 Major Schenck was a member of the Assembly and up to the time of his death he fulfilled the duties of a useful and public-spirited citizen.

General Washington and Abraham Yates, while attending the Fishkill Convention, were entertained by the Major and Mrs. Schenck and later, when the Commander-in-Chief had his headquarters at Newburgh, he was a welcome guest at Locust Grove. The Marquis de la Fayette likewise enjoyed the hospitality of the Schenck household, as did also Baron von Steuben, who had his headquarters at Mount Gulian nearby.

In 1790 Alice Schenck married Isaac de Peyster Teller and they began housekeeping in the large brick house on the Fish Kill, built by Abraham de Peyster in 1743, when he bought the mill property from Madame Brett. This Mr. Teller had inherited from his great-uncle Abraham. There they lived for several years until they moved up to Locust Grove. After Major Schenck's death, Mr. Teller bought the homestead from the "doweress," as Madame Schenck was called, who thereafter continued to live with her daughter and son-in-law. *"With the genius of wise farming,"* Isaac Teller *"developed the property until it became locally renowned for its grain and other farm products."* The economic system of slave labour, however, apparently did not wholly commend itself to him. Once, when the old Dutch Dominie came to call, Mr. Teller was just setting forth on his accustomed rounds of the farm and took the Dominie along with him. As they came back to the house the Dominie, much impressed by what he had seen, said,

PLATE 46   ZEBULON SOUTHARD HOUSE, FISHKILL: SOUTH FRONT   NO. 21 ON MAP

"Mr. Teller, you must be a very rich man."

"No, Dominie," said Mr. Teller, "I'm not. I'm a poor man."

"But, Mr. Teller, with all these acres of corn land, all these fine, fat swine, and all these negro slaves, how can you be poor?"

"That's just it, Dominie, I'm a poor man."

"But I don't understand."

"Well, Dominie, it's this way. The hogs eat up all the corn, and the damned niggers eat up all the hogs!" *

The Honourable Isaac de Peyster Teller, as a member of Congress and a country squire, was highly esteemed and beloved. Kindly and generous by nature, he was especially considerate of the poor who lived on the mountain lands.

When there was no Episcopal church nearer than Fishkill village, Miss Hannah Teller, aided by her sisters, established a mission in the "long room"—the dining-room—of the house. To get a clergyman, in winter Mr. Teller would drive on the ice to West Point to fetch the Reverend Mr. Hackley, then Chaplain of the Post. Later on, as the mission grew, a corner of the orchard was given for the purpose and a chapel built. The mission was put in charge of the Reverend Robert Boyd Van Kleeck, son of Dr. Baltus Livingston Van Kleeck of Newburgh. This young parson found a wife in Miss Margaret Teller. Their daughter's descendant still lives in

this old house of many memories. In the spring of 1939 the National Society of Colonial Dames in the State of New York placed upon the outer wall of the Homestead a bronze tablet in honour of Madame Brett. "In grateful recognition of her service in this Community."

In 1792, when he and Mrs. Teller had moved up to the Teller Homestead, Isaac de Peyster Teller sold the ABRAHAM DE PEYSTER HOUSE (Plate 41) on the creek to William Byrnes, who took into partnership Cyrus Newlin of Wilmington, Delaware. Until 1811 Mr. Byrnes and Mr. Newlin conducted the mill property together; then Mr. Newlin bought Mr. Byrnes's interests. Cyrus Newlin did not live in Fishkill, but his sons, Robert and Isaac, lived in the de Peyster house and, as the Newlin family occupied it for a long time, it was often called the Newlin house. It is now in a dilapidated state.

It was not until about 1737 that MOUNT GULIAN (Plate 43)—the house that was to witness the birth of the Society of Cincinnati—was built on the third part of the Rombout Patent that fell to the Verplanck family and was developed later than Madame Brett's portion. In 1730 another Gulian Verplanck had came into possession of the estate and, since he married in 1737, it seems likely that he built his

*Since the original text has not been altered in this edition, this anecdote has been preserved intact despite its unfortunate racism.

PLATE 47   HENDRICK KIP HOUSE, FISHKILL: NORTH FRONT   No. 20 ON MAP

PLATE 48   CORNELIUS VAN WYCK HOUSE ("WHARTON HOUSE"), FISHKILL: NO. 22 ON MAP
SOUTH FRONT

country house just before or just after that important event in his life. It is said the house was built largely by the labour of his own slaves. Whoever planned the structure, the gambrel roof—flaring outward bell-wise at the foot of the lower pitch to form the verandah roof, on both the east and west fronts —was one of the best examples of this manner of construction anywhere to be found. The higher northern part of the house Daniel Crommelin Verplanck added in 1804, when it became necessary to enlarge the original building.

The rooms in the old part were spacious and comfortable but unpretentious in character. In the new part, however, there was a ball room said to have been exactly copied after the State Dining-room at the White House in Washington. East of the ball room was the dining-room, at one time used as a bedroom. The Marquis de la Fayette so used it when he visited Mount Gulian in 1824; ever after it was known as the La Fayette Room. To the north was the kitchen. The entrance was on the east front of the older part and admitted to a wide stair hall running through to the west. To the right was a broad hall—really a long room in its proportions and in the manner of its use—giving access to the Cincinnati Room and also to the 1804 enlargement.

The upper floor, although from the outside apparently of very limited proportions, was really surprisingly capacious.

The most memorable incident connected with Mount Gulian was the institution of the Society of the Cincinnati. In the room on the ground floor whose windows overlooked the Hudson—always thereafter known as the Cincinnati Room—on Tuesday, May 13, 1783, was organised this famous society which has been perpetuated ever since, despite periods of opposition and indifference. In the Cincinnati Room the original beamed ceiling had been laid bare, after being long covered with lath and plaster, so that its latter condition was the same as when the Society was organised there.

Samuel Verplanck, to whom his father Gulian left Mount Gulian, married Judith Crommelin. During the Revolutionary War, while the British forces occupied New York City, Judith Verplanck often entertained Lord Howe at their town house beside old City Hall. As souvenirs of this hospitality, Lord Howe gave his hostess some paintings by Angelica Kauffmann and a tea set, treasured by the Verplanck descendants. Whilst Samuel and Judith Verplanck were living in their town house, General Baron von Steuben occupied Mount Gulian as his headquarters

PLATE 49   DUTCH REFORMED CHURCH, FISHKILL: SOUTH SIDE AND EAST END   NO. 23 ON MAP

for at least a part of the war period. Thence he could readily go to supervise the tactical and disciplinary training of the American troops quartered near Fishkill; he could also easily cross the river to Newburgh when Washington had his headquarters there.

It has been said that Samuel Verplanck was a Loyalist, but too good care was taken of Mount Gulian to make it likely that he was actively so; there are no recorded proceedings against him under the Act of Forfeiture, as there almost certainly would have been if he had openly maintained allegiance to the Crown. After the declaration of peace, Samuel and Judith Verplanck returned to Mount Gulian. Although the house itself had sustained no injury, there were many claims to adjust with reference to the farm, especially in the matter of compensation for timber felled. Eventually the place regained its wonted aspect of peace and order, and family life resumed its accustomed placid routine.

Daniel Crommelin Verplanck, the son of Samuel

and Judith, inherited Mount Gulian. He was a member of Congress and also Judge of the County. He kept open house at Mount Gulian, summer and winter, and holidays brought an host of visitors. The rooms were filled with beautiful furniture, fine paintings and other objects of elegance, many of which the Judge's mother, Judith Crommelin, had brought from Holland. The Judge himself was a great collector of silver. He was also a good judge of wine and had a fine stock of Madeira he had laid down in 1804 when he enlarged the house. For many years all the old customs were maintained at Mount Gulian, including the three o'clock dinner hour.

Daniel Crommelin Verplanck and his daughter Mary Anna were ardent gardeners and they themselves laid out the gardens and grounds immediately about the house. Box bushes, trees and shrubs they planted are still flourishing. It is one of the traditions of Mount Gulian that Daniel Crommelin planted all the streams in the neighbourhood with

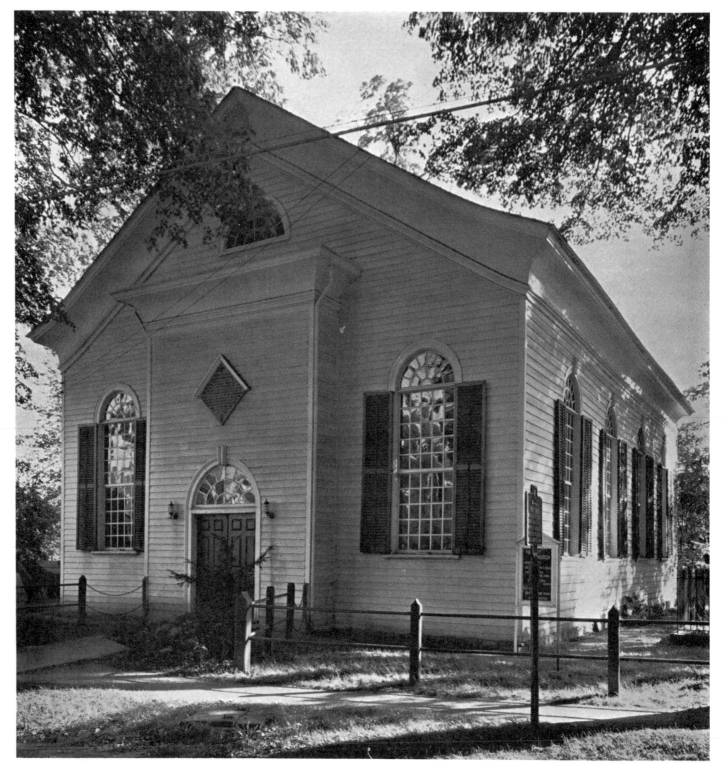

PLATE 52

TRINITY CHURCH, FISHKILL: NORTH FRONT

PLATE 54   "PLENTY ACRES" (STORM-ADRIANCE-BRINCKERHOFF HOUSE),   NO. 28 ON MAP
UPPER HOPEWELL: SOUTH FRONT

PLATE 55   MESIER HOMESTEAD, MESIER PARK, WAPPINGERS FALLS: NO. 30 ON MAP
SOUTH FRONT

PLATE 56 VERPLANCK-VAN WYCK HOUSE, FISHKILL PLAINS: WEST END NO. 29 ON MAP

watercress, by seed brought from Washington when he was a member of Congress. James Brown, the black gardener, was one of the institutions of the place. A runaway slave from Maryland, Mr. Verplanck had afterwards purchased his freedom from his former master. He presided over the garden from 1829 until 1864, when he died "full of years and honours." He had learned to read and write and during all this period he kept a diary in which he noted down the names of all visitors to Mount Gulian and his comments upon them. This diary grew to the bulk of seven volumes.

The CHRYSTIE HOUSE (Plate 44) at Beacon was built about 1821 by Albert Chrystie and is characterised by the excellent proportions and graceful details typical of that era. Mr. Chrystie married Colonel William Few's daughter. Born in Maryland in 1748, William Few had removed to Georgia in 1776, and he represented Georgia in the Conti-

nental Congress; he was also one of the Georgia Executive Council. He was a judge, and later a United States Senator from Georgia and *"was complimented with nearly every prominent office within the gift of his adopted State."* In 1799 he removed to New York City and was occupied with public duties and banking interests. In July, 1828, he died at Mr. Chrystie's house and was buried at Fishkill.

The house was sold in 1833 and Dr. Rumsey lived there for many years; his daughters finally sold it in 1924. Not long afterwards, Dr. C. J. Slocum bought it and moved it to its present site for his own residence in the grounds of his sanatorium.

The ZEBULON SOUTHARD HOUSE (Plate 46) near Fishkill village, on the north side of the road from Beacon, is arresting in its sturdy Batavian simplicity. Zebulon Southard, who built the house about 1766, was afterwards Captain in a Dutchess County regiment that served during the Revolution. It is worth noting that the walls are clapboarded over an inner

PLATE 58   THE GLEBE HOUSE, MAIN STREET, POUGHKEEPSIE: SOUTH FRONT   NO. 35 ON MAP

thick lath cribwork filled with a hardset stiff mixture of clay and straw, re-enforced with cornstalks.

Nearby, facing north on the opposite side of the road, is the HENDRICK KIP HOUSE (Plate 47), a one-and-a-half storey stone structure (at some time painted red) of unmistakably Dutch ancestry. In its present form (save for an extension at the back and some modernisations in front) it stands as built by Hendrick Kip in 1753, although in all likelihood James Hussey, who owned the place at that time, built the eastern part about 1720. Hendrick Kip, born in 1688, was the son of Hendrick Kip and spent his boyhood in his father's house, Kipsbergen, at Rhinecliff. After Hendrick Kip's death in 1754, the house passed through various hands. Baron von Steuben had his headquarters there for a part of the time while he was training the troops at Fishkill during the Revolutionary War. The present owner is William Hammond.

Cornelius Van Wyck built the VAN WYCK HOUSE (Plate 48) (called "Wharton House" on the roadside marker) early in the 18th century; the larger western end was added before 1757. It is on the east side of the Post Road, about a mile south of Fishkill village. Historic associations of undoubted authenticity cluster about this house; also other associations of romantic flavour that may or may not have a background of fact. Evidence is lacking either to substantiate or disallow the latter; we may take them for what they are worth. Fenimore Cooper, in *The Spy*, where fact and fiction are blended, called this the "Wharton House," supposedly the home of a family that had removed thither during the Revolution after their house in Westchester County was burnt. He also made Harvey Birch, the American spy, pilot Captain Wharton of the British Army here to visit his family, next relating how the Americans captured Captain Wharton and held him prisoner until, by Birch's aid, he escaped through neutral ground to the British lines near New York.

PLATE 59   THE GLEBE HOUSE, MAIN STREET, POUGHKEEPSIE: PARLOUR

The original of Harvey Birch in the novel was Enoch Crosby in real life. Crosby led an exciting life as a spy during the war. He seems to have been able to insinuate himself into the confidence of both the British and American authorities; whenever he was captured, influence from high quarters secured his immediate release. Though frequently serving the purposes of the British military command, he was really in the American secret service, and always carried credentials that procured his freedom whenever captured by American troops. Crosby's actual connection with the Van Wyck house was this: He lured a company of Loyalists there, in 1776, where the Whigs seized them and turned them over for trial by the Committee of Safety. On another occasion he decoyed a group of Loyalists to Fishkill where they were all arrested, Crosby included, and tried together, and were then confined in the old DUTCH CHURCH (Plate 49), used as a military gaol. Crosby's detention, however, was short; the local authorities, given a hint that his imprisonment was not desired, connived at his escape from a window of the church. The particular window is still pointed out.

During the Revolution there were large encampments at Fishkill. It was a gathering place and base of supplies, and some military manufactures were carried on. The barracks extended along the Post Road and were close to the Van Wyck house, which General Israel Putnam and other high officers from time to time made their headquarters. It was also the scene of several courts-martial. Nearby is the plot where many of the Revolutionary soldiers who died in the encampment were buried. A more cheerful memory is that of Isaac Van Wyck, a member of the State Legislature in 1794, 1796, 1810 and 1811, who always travelled to the sessions in his large yellow coach, with negro coachman and footman.

"SHILLELAGH" (Plate 50), on the north side of the main village street of Fishkill, was built about 1811 by James Given of Cullybackey in Ireland who, a few years before, had settled in Fishkill and become a prosperous merchant. Some unrecorded sentiment seems to have impelled the owner to bestow the name Shillelagh on his home, probably to perpetuate the name of the town near his birthplace. Tradition says that when the house was finished *"a bottle of wine was thrown over it."* The bottle did not

PLATE 60   VAN KEUREN HOUSE, NEAR POUGHKEEPSIE: WEST OR RIVER FRONT   NO. 33 ON MAP

PLATE 61   OLD HUNDRED, NEW HACKENSACK: SOUTH FRONT   NO. 31 ON MAP

break and, therefore, according to ancient superstition, the house would never burn.

Shillelagh is typical of the better sort of wooden house built in Dutchess County in the Federal Era and is thought to be the work of the same architect-carpenter who fashioned the equally engaging RAPALJE-BLODGETT HOUSE (Plate 51), about 1800. This house, east of the Post Road and just south of the Fish Kill, built for Richard Rapalje and renovated for Mr. and Mrs. Blodgett, the present owners, has no distinctive name like Shillelagh. The lack recalls an anecdote told by Mr. Blodgett. At the time of building, it was customary for the master carpenter-architect and his prentices to be quartered "on the job" during the final stages of work. In this case, according to local story, when they were ready to "hoist the bush" as a symbol of completion, the craftsman dubbed the house "Starvation Hall"—said he'd not had one decent meal there during his whole contract. He may, of course, have had indigestion, or an inordinate appetite. At any rate, one can understand why the occupants to-day decline to revive the name.

TRINITY CHURCH (Plate 52), in Fishkill Village, was built about 1769, although the Church of England congregation was organised by the Reverend Samuel Seabury in 1756. The church building was occupied by the New York Provincial Convention in September, 1776, after they removed from the Odell house at Hartsdale, near White Plains. The church also served as a military hospital during part of the Revolutionary War.

The JOHN BRINCKERHOFF HOUSE (Plate 53), east of Fishkill village and south of the road to Hopewell, is the stone dwelling John Brinckerhoff built in 1738. Dr. Theodorus Van Wyck, who had married the daughter of the family and lived also in the house, sat as a delegate in the third Provincial Congress and rendered useful public services during the Revolutionary War. Late in 1778 General Washington occasionally stayed at the house and tradition says that the *motherly Mrs. Brinckerhoff* herself saw *that the Commander-in-Chief was warmly tucked up in his bed on the cold autumn nights.* Tradition relates also that Brinckerhoff once questioned Washington about military conditions. The General asked Brinckerhoff if he could keep a secret, to which Brinckerhoff replied he could. Said Washington, *"So can I."*

The STORM - ADRIANCE - BRINCKERHOFF HOUSE (Plate 54), (now called "Plenty Acres"), at Upper Hopewell also has Washington associations. The lower western part of the house must have been built soon after Dirck Hegeman bought the land in 1759, cleared it and began farming. In 1769 Garret

Storm bought the farm and gave it to his son Thomas, who married in 1771 and is thought to have built the higher eastern part near that time. Both parts have undergone some changes since then.

Thomas Storm was a Captain in the Second Regiment of Dutchess County Militia in the Revolutionary War and sat in the State Assembly from 1781 to 1784. In 1785 he moved to New York City, which he represented in the State Legislature from 1798 to 1803. He was also a candidate for the Lieutenant-Governourship. While he lived at Upper Hopewell during the Revolution, the road passing his house was a main highway between the South and New England, for the British held New York. One of the many distinguished travellers using this road was Washington and once, when he had spent the night at Captain Storm's, in the morning a gathering of the neighbours standing with bared heads before the door greeted him. The General, annoyed or embarrassed, bade them put their hats on—'*he also was a man.*' Captain Storm was chairman of the local vigilance committee during the Revolution and is said at various times to have confined military prisoners in the cellar until they could be finally dealt with. In 1785 Storm's brother-in-law, John Adriance, bought the house and, until recently, it passed from one to another of the Storm, Adriance and Brinckerhoff kindred.

The MESIER HOMESTEAD (Plate 55), as it is known, standing in Mesier Park at Wappingers Falls, was built about 1750 by Nicholas Brouwer or Brewer. In 1777, Peter Mesier, a prospering New York merchant, wishing to be in a less tempestuous place, left the city and bought this house, in part of which, it is said, he kept a general store. Mesier was a Loyalist. Though politically inactive and peaceable, his sympathies were anathema to the excited local Whigs. On three successive days in May, 1777, just after he had moved in, Whig rowdies (under colour of protesting the price of his tea) broke into the house, beat Mesier and his slaves and drank the wine in his cellar. Changes were made in the house early in the 19th century and again during the "Hudson River Gothic" vogue. The Mesier family continued as occupants until 1891, when the house and immediate grounds passed into the ownership of the village for park purposes.

The VERPLANCK-VAN WYCK HOUSE (Plate 56) built by Philip Verplanck, jr., in 1768 at Fishkill Plains, where the road from Hopewell to Poughkeepsie crosses the Sprout Creek, is a roomy gambrel-roofed brick dwelling. About 1722, on his land in the Rombout Patent, Gulian Verplanck built a mill and dwelling on the Sprout Creek. Before his death in 1745 the mill had become such an important commercial centre for all the neighbouring

PLATE 62 PROSPECT HILL, FREEDOM PLAINS: SOUTH FRONT

farm region that a road had to be made thence to the Hudson and "Farmers' Landing" established at the mouth of Wappingers Creek for the shipment of produce. As a very young man Philip Verplanck jr. went into residence at Sprout Creek and conducted the business of the mill and the landing. In 1764 he married Aefje, daughter of Gerard Beekman, and in 1768 built the present house. His heirs sold it in 1827 to Richard C. Van Wyck, from whom it descended to the present owners. No exciting historical events are associated with the house but, besides being an admirable example of 18th-century domestic architecture, it is an eloquent reminder of the significant part played by grist mills in the development of the country.

The CLEAR EVERITT HOUSE (Plate 57), on Main Street, Poughkeepsie, was built about 1770, either by Clear Everitt, former Sheriff of the County, or his brother Richard. Richard Everitt was a Loyalist; whether Clear Everitt was a Loyalist is not definitely

known. He seems to have been away from Poughkeepsie during at least part of the Revolutionary War. His house, in any event, was used for various public purposes. One of the courts for a time sat in one of the rooms, for in the minutes of the Supervisors, for June 1, 1784, is the following:

"To Clear Everitt for the use of his room for the use of the Court of Oyer and Terminer to set in June, 1778, £2."

Besides this use of the property, of which there is definite record, there is strong and persistent tradition associating the house with the Revolutionary leaders. Governour Clinton seems to have occupied it at some time during his residence in Poughkeepsie. Also, the following from the Loyalist *New York Gazette*, of July 4, 1781, apparently points to the Everitt house:

"There is a set of mob legislators met at Poughkeepsie; a little time will shew whether they mean to expose themselves to all the vengeance of which the majority of the late Assembly and Senate live in constant dread, many of them changing

PLATE 64   BRICK HOUSE FARM, PLEASANT VALLEY:
GENERAL VIEW FROM DUCK POND

PLATE 66   MORRIS GRAHAM HOUSE (THE OLD STONE HOUSE), PINE PLAINS: NO. 48 ON MAP
FROM SOUTHWEST

PLATE 67   GERMOND HILL, MILLBROOK: SOUTH FRONT   No. 37 ON MAP

their lodgings to elude the search of the avengers of the innocent blood they have shed. Mr. Clinton, the titular Governour, has fortified his hut against a sudden surprise, and the rebel slaves of Poughkeepsie guard it every night."

In his *History of Dutchess County*, Philip Smith, after the word "hut," interpolates "the fine stone mansion of Clear Everitt."

Whether Governour Clinton did or did not then take up residence there, if Clear Everitt was away from Poughkeepsie, the Revolutionary leaders certainly used his house in some way, *"for they had need of all the buildings they could obtain, as the little town"*—the capital of the State for the time being—*"was often crowded with distinguished visitors during the sessions of the Legislature."* That Washington and la Fayette were entertained there is not unlikely. The house has been called "'The old fort,' the 'Headquarters' and the 'prison house,' with probably some reason for all three."* The Poughkeepsie gaol could not possibly have held all the Loyalist

prisoners sent for detention, nor was it usual to confine well-known and respectable persons in gaol if it could be avoided.

In 1767 the members of Christ Church, Poughkeepsie, subscribed to buy a glebe and GLEBE HOUSE (Plate 58) for the Rector of their parish. Glebe land and house were on what is now Main Street. The first occupant of the house was the Reverend John Beardsley who, when the Revolutionary War broke out, was a Loyalist and, with other Loyalist refugees, went to New York City. Upon the evacuation of New York by the British Army, he went to New Brunswick in Canada and there continued as a missionary. During the war, while the parish was without a Rector, two staff officers with duties in Poughkeepsie, successively rented the Glebe House. From 1787 to 1791 the Reverend Henry Van Dyck was incumbent of Christ Church and occupied the Glebe House. In 1792 the church sold house and land, and

it was during the ownership of Peter De Reimer that his daughter eloped from one of the windows. The house now belongs to the City of Poughkeepsie and is in custody of the Junior League.

The VAN KEUREN HOUSE (Plate 60), at the mouth of a little stream the Dutch called *Speck zyn Kil,* about 4 miles south of Poughkeepsie, has now little architectural attraction—ground floor and basement alone retain traces of its original aspect—but it recalls bits of diverting history. Matthew Van Keuren built it about 1730 or 1735; besides running his mill, he kept a ferry. Nearby was a forge where, in Revolutionary times, some of the links in the chain stretched across the river to Fort Montgomery are said to have been wrought. In October 1777—the house then belonged to Theophilus Anthony—when the British sailed up the river on their raiding expedition, some of the men came ashore to burn the buildings at *Speck zyn Kil.* The Anthony family fled to the woods, but the slave Dinah stayed in the

kitchen where she had just finished baking bread. The raiders fired the mill but Dinah's persuasive talk, baited with fragrant hot loaves, coaxed them to leave the house untouched.

OLD HUNDRED (Plate 61), at New Hackensack, built about 1755 or 1760, boasts no significant history but displays such architectural poise and characteristics of such sterling suggestive merit that it well deserves illustration. Its clapboarded walls are filled in with clay in which hair is mixed.

PROSPECT HILL (Plate 62), near Freedom Plains, was built about 1788 by Gilbert R. Livingston on land he had received from his father, inherited through his grandmother, Cornelia Beekman. During the Revolution, Gilbert Livingston was one of the few Loyalists in a conspicuously Whig family. Judge Thomas Jones, in his *History of New York,* speaks of Gilbert as *"a lad of spirit."* About 1781, when he was twenty-three, he held a commission in a

75

PLATE 69

SPRINGWOOD, HYDE PARK: EAST FRONT

NO. 39 ON MAP

Loyalist regiment. He married Martha Kane, daughter of John Kane, also a Loyalist. The quietude and remoteness of Prospect Hill were probably not unwelcome in the immediate post-war period while anti-British sentiment was still acute in the Hudson Valley. Gilbert Livingston sold Prospect Hill in 1797 to General Augustus Barker who, in turn, sold it in 1819 to Philip J. Schuyler of The Grove, at Rhinebeck. The present owners are Mr. and Mrs. Frank D. Roylance.

BRICK HOUSE FARM (Plate 63), in the town of Pleasant Valley, is a satisfying piece of Georgian architecture dating from about 1778. Sarah Tobias Newcomb capably superintended the building of the house while her husband, Zaccheus Newcomb, was away in the Continental Army. The ends of the beam-anchors in the west wall are so shaped that they can be read as "Z" or, in reverse, as "N"—Zaccheus Newcomb's initials. The bricks for the house were burned on the place and the pit from which they dug the brick clay is now the duck pond. The present owners are Mr. and Mrs. John Adams Brown; Mrs. Brown is a direct descendant of Zaccheus Newcomb.

The MARK ROW HOUSE (Plate 65), near Rock City, was built in 1818 by Mark Rau or Row on land his father, Johannes Rau, had acquired in 1760. While not significant historically, the house is noteworthy for the beauty and delicacy of rather unusual exterior woodwork details.

The bachelor who built himself the little stone MORRIS GRAHAM HOUSE (Plate 66) between Halcyon Lake and the village of Pine Plains in 1772, moved to Dutchess from Westchester County to look after land-holdings he had inherited there. His maternal grandfather was Lewis Morris, Lord of the Manor of Morrisania, and Lewis Morris the "Signer" was his cousin. His paternal grandfather was Augustine Graham, who had been Surveyor-General of the Province from 1691 to 1719 and was one of the nine grantees of the Little Nine Partners' Patent in Dutchess County. In 1775, soon after Morris Graham had settled on his holdings derived from the partition of the Little Nine Partners' Patent, he represented Dutchess County at the Provincial Convention in New York City and, in 1775 and 1776, was a Dutchess County delegate to the Second and Third Provincial Congresses. He became Colonel of a regiment of Dutchess County Militia and is said to have spent nearly all his means in keeping a full complement of his men in the field and adequately equipped. After the War, he went to Deerfield, in Oneida County, and died there at his sister's home about 1805.

The house at GERMOND HILL (Plate 67), built (it would seem) about 1800, faces south from a hilltop between Verbank and Millbrook (just within the southern limit of the old Great Nine Partners' Patent). From this vantage point there is a panoramic view of vast extent and exceptional diversity—an enduring witness to the imagination of the original builders in choosing such a site instead of seeking the more customary shelter in the lee of a hillside. The family of James Germond, who settled there in the 18th century, apparently bore the name Germaine originally, but the Huguenot "Germaine," in travelling from France by way of Barbadoes and Long Island, finally became "Germond" in Dutchess County and is now perpetuated thus in the name of the estate. There have been additions and some alterations to the house in recent years. The Germonds sold the place in 1905. The present owners are Mr. and Mrs. G. R. Collins.

About 1760, David Johnstone, of New York City, built LITHGOW (Plate 68) as a countryseat. His mother, from whom he inherited the land, was the daughter of David Jamison of Linlithgow, in Scotland, who came to America in the latter part of the 17th century. Sometime Chief-Justice of New Jersey, Secretary and Attorney-General of the Province of New York, and a Warden of Trinity Church, in 1697 David Jamison was one of the grantees of the Great Nine Partners' Patent in Dutchess County. It was a portion of this land of David Jamison's that descended to David Johnstone, the builder of Lithgow, David Johnstone was twice President of St. Andrew's Society and was one of the Committee appointed to welcome Washington at his triumphal entry into New York City in 1783. After the death of David Johnstone and other members of his family, Lithgow was sold in 1813 to Judge Isaac Smith, whose great-grandson, Isaac Smith Wheaton later became the owner.

The original or central part of SPRINGWOOD (Plate 69) at Hyde Park, the Dutchess County home of President Roosevelt, was built between 1833 and 1835 by Joseph Giraud who demolished a much dilapidated 18th-century house on or near the site. The 1833-35 house passed through several ownerships until President Roosevelt's grandfather bought it in 1868. The house was formerly clapboarded over brick; eventually the clapboard casing gave place to stucco and large stone wings were added at the north and south ends. Architecturally impressive, Springwood is historically significant both as the family home of a President of the United States and because of visits by the King and Queen, and many distinguished guests besides, both royal and otherwise, who have been entertained there.

PLATE 70 ROBERT SANDS HOUSE, RHINEBECK: EAST END

PLATE 72   THE BEEKMAN ARMS, RHINEBECK: EAST FRONT   No. 44 ON MAP

PLATE 73   GLENBURN, RHINEBECK: SOUTH FRONT   No. 43 ON MAP

PLATE 74   WILDERCLIFF, RHINECLIFF: SOUTH FRONT   No. 40 ON MAP

PLATE 75   WILDERCLIFF, RHINECLIFF: DINING ROOM

Two houses on Landsman's Kill, about a mile and a half east of Rhinebeck, are closely linked in their history—THE GROVE (Plate 71), built by Philip J. Schuyler (son of General Philip Schuyler) about 1795, and ROBERT SANDS'S HOUSE (Plate 70) (known also as the Bowne house) built about 1796.

Before 1740 Jacob Rutsen had a stone house on the rise above his mill and, after his early death, his widow (Alida Livingston) continued there and managed the large estate for their infant son John. When John came of age, he married and had two daughters, but died about 1771 when only twenty-eight. In 1779 his widow married Robert Sands, who added river transportation and other interests to the mill business, and was as good a father to the two little Rutsen girls as he was to his own children who followed. When Sarah, the younger of John Rutsen's daughters, married Philip J. Schuyler, the stone house on the hill became too small for the combined families and was torn down, to be replaced by two houses. Both houses have always remained in pos-

session of the Schuyler and Sands descendants. The Sands house, now belonging to Mr. and Mrs. Rupert Anderson, is unchanged save for some minor verandah additions. The Grove, now the home of Mr. and Mrs. Malcolm E. Smith, has been greatly enlarged, but consistently with its original character. One of the treasured possessions at The Grove is the great black walnut tree west of the house, planted by General Schuyler on one of his visits to his son.

The BEEKMAN ARMS (Plate 72) at Rhinebeck began as the one-storey two-room stone house William Traphagen built about 1700. His son, Arendt Traphagen, enlarged the house until, in 1769, it was two full storeys high with an attic and *"included the parts enclosed by the heavy stone walls of the present building."* Subsequent enlargements to meet requirements of increased patronage are easily discernible, but the older part preserves its original character. History a-plenty centres about the inn, and memories of the eminent personages who have

PLATE 76   ABRAHAM KIP HOUSE, RHINECLIFF: SOUTH FRONT   No. 41 ON MAP

frequented it—Washington, la Fayette, General Schuyler, General Montgomery, General Armstrong, Alexander Hamilton, Arnold, De Witt Clinton, Silas Wright, Martin Van Buren, to name only a few —but a single incident must suffice for illustration:

> "There is the identical fireplace [in the dining-room] before which one night in 1813 Aaron Burr and General John Armstrong sat chatting when Miss Eliza Jacques, daughter of the landlord, entered to pass through to the kitchen. Burr, who had just returned from the French court, imperiously ordered her to bring him a boot-jack. She modestly replied: 'It is not my place to bring you a boot-jack but I will order a servant to do it.' Burr sprang up angrily and shaking his fist at her, shouted: 'By God! you are not too good to bring me a boot-jack!' General Armstrong sprang in front of Burr and shaking his fist in turn at him, cried: 'By God, sir, she is too good to bring you a boot-jack, and if you say that again I'll knock you down, sir!' Burr subsided."

GLENBURN (Plate 73) near Rhinebeck is another of the Dutchess County places that has never been sold but has descended to the present owner in a direct line by inheritance. It is part of the original Beekman grant. From Margaret Beekman, who married Judge Livingston of Clermont, this portion of the grant passed to her namesake daughter who married Dr. Thomas Tillotson. From their share of the Beekman grant, Dr. Tillotson, in 1830, gave his granddaughter, Julia M. Lynch, the 66 acres of Glenburn because *as a child she used to play in the stream and the falls and asked her grandfather to give it to her.* The house was built about 1830; there Stephen Olin and his family, the Lynchs and Montgomerys spent their summers. Since 1830 the house has been changed and enlarged several times. The last change was made in 1937 for the present owner, Olin Dows, grandson of Stephen H. Olin.

WILDERCLIFF (Plate 74) stands on a high wooded bluff below Rhinecliff and commands a long view southward over the Hudson and its valley. The house was built in 1799 and occupied by the Reverend Freeborn Garretson and his wife, Catharine Livingston; their only child, Miss Mary Garretson, continued to live there until her death in 1879. Wildercliff is now the home of Mrs. E. D. Hawkins.

Born in 1752 of a Church of England family in Maryland, Mr. Garretson as a young man embraced Methodism, in 1776 entered the Methodist ministry, becoming a circuit-rider and, from 1817 until his death in 1827, pursued his missionary labours as a volunteer. In 1793 he married Catharine Livingston, the Chancellor's one remaining single sister, who had lived on at Clermont with her widowed mother after her five sisters had successively married and gone to homes of their own. There is a family legend that Catharine Livingston one day stood at the window and said she was going to marry the next man that came up the drive. The next man was Freeborn Garretson.

Notwithstanding their utterly dissimilar backgrounds, personalities and tastes, the marriage was singularly happy and the home they created

> "was the scene of unlimited hospitality, not only to friends and family but to all who needed temporary shelter. It was a haven, where all sorts and conditions of humanity found aid and comfort."

The ABRAHAM KIP HOUSE (Plate 76), an early 18th-century stone dwelling, stands at the fork of the road from Rhinebeck to Rhinecliff. The south fork goes on to Rhinecliff village; the right, which keeps on westward and passes directly in front of the house, is part of the old Sepasco Trail from the river to Rhinebeck. At its river end was a ferry to Kingston and there was so much east and west travel over this road, and so many travellers seeking shelter or refreshment, that Abraham Kip's house became virtually an inn. A little to the south, on the east side of the road to Rhinecliff, are the ruins of Kipsbergen, the house Hendrick Kip (Abraham's uncle) built at the beginning of the 18th century, afterwards owned by the Beekmans and Livingstons. It was probably at Kipsbergen the Van Cortlandts stayed when they had to leave the Manor House at Croton during the Revolutionary War.

ANKONY (Plate 77), perpetuating the name of an Indian chief, is the summer home of the Honourable Allan A. Ryan, Jr. The house stands a little to the north of the Abraham Kip house and overlooks the river. Dating from the fore part of the 19th century, it well exemplifies the spacious mien and poise that characterised much of the domestic architecture in the Greek Revival period.

MONTGOMERY PLACE (Plate 78) at Barrytown, overlooking the Hudson, is the house Mrs. Richard Montgomery, widow of Major-General Montgomery, built between 1802 and 1805.

Richard Montgomery, resigning his captaincy in the British Army, came to New York in 1772 and not long afterwards married Janet Livingston, Chancellor Livingston's sister. They had just begun to build a house south of Rhinebeck when, at the outbreak of war, Captain Montgomery, whose sympathies were wholly with the Colonies, entered the Continental Army with a Brigadier-General's commission, rapidly followed by promotion to a Major-Generalcy. The story of his death at the head of his troops before Quebec, December 31, 1775, is well known to all. After that, Mrs. Montgomery finished the house they had begun near Rhinebeck but, because of its sad associations, she sold it and built Montgomery Place. The north pavilion, west verandah and south wing were added in 1844; the east

PLATE 79   MONTGOMERY PLACE, BARRYTOWN: WEST FRONT

PLATE 80 MONTGOMERY PLACE, BARRYTOWN: DINING ROOM

portico, terrace, roof balustrade and considerable exterior ornament date from the 1860's. The interior of the original part of the house remains as it was in 1805, and much of Mrs. Montgomery's furniture is still there. Mrs. Montgomery had no children and since her death (in 1828) Montgomery Place has gone from one to another of her kindred. General John Ross Delafield, the present owner, descends in one line from Chancellor Livingston and, in another, from Mrs. Montgomery's sister.

ROKEBY (Plate 81), first called *La Bergerie,* is the house below Barrytown General John Armstrong of the Continental Army (author of the "Newburgh Letters") built in 1815. The Armstrongs moved into this house "on top of the carpenters." In March, 1815, the General wrote a friend:

> "I have been entirely occupied devising ways and means to make my family comfortable in their new quarters. We were driven out of our old ones [the house burned down] rather prematurely, and with a loss, the extent of which every day makes us better acquainted with. Of my papers all were saved excepting one box. . . . We are tolerably lodged in the new house and have the music of saws and hammers to wake us at daybreak."

Between 1790 and 1800 General Armstrong, who had married Alida, Chancellor Livingston's youngest sister, lived at various places in the neighbourhood. From 1800 to 1804, while he was in the United States Senate, he is said to have lived at Kingston so that his children might be educated there. In 1804 he became Minister to France and, in 1811, on his return from Europe, he selected the site for a house of considerable size near Barrytown and settled in one of his cottages while the future Rokeby was a-building and a Scottish carpenter was carrying out his instructions. It was from this cottage that fire drove the General and his family into the yet unfinished house.

Mr. William B. Astor, who married the Armstrongs' only daughter, succeeded them as owner and thereafter spent every summer (save one, which he passed in Europe) at Rokeby, to which Mrs. Astor gave the name after reading Scott's poem. Mrs. Margaret Chanler Aldrich, the present owner, is a great-grandchild who, with her nine brothers and sisters, was taken to live at Rokeby in 1876, a few months after Mr. Astor's death. In the nineteenth century Rokeby experienced sundry additions and

Plate 82 Edgewater, Barrytown: West Front

PLATE 83   CALLENDAR HOUSE, BARRYTOWN: WEST FRONT   No. 50 ON MAP

PLATE 84   CALLENDAR HOUSE, BARRYTOWN: EAST FRONT

PLATE 85 MAIZEFIELD, RED HOOK: EAST FRONT

changes, but preserves untouched much of the exquisite design and detail of the Federal Era, especially indoors where, as Mr. Astor often said, *"Warner Richards made every panel in this house with his own hands."* Some of the beautiful furniture General Armstrong brought back from France is still in the house.

EDGEWATER (Plate 82), near Barrytown, was built in 1820 for Mrs. Lowndes Brown by her father, John R. Livingston. It was the second owner, Robert Donaldson, who engaged the well-known architect, Alexander Davis, to design the library. About 1903 Mrs. John Jay Chapman bought Edgewater from Mr. Donaldson's daughter. From Mrs. Chapman the house came to the present owner, Mr. Conrad Chapman.

Edgewater, as may be gathered from the illustration, is instinct with the combined dignity and subtle grace that marked the houses of the Federal Era before the excess of archaeological propriety and gravity of the Greek Revival had made so much of our domestic architecture forget how to smile. Not the least pleasant feature of Edgewater is to be found in the twin gazebos with umbrella roofs that mark each end of a little cove making in from the river just south of the house.

CALLENDAR HOUSE (Plate 83), between Tivoli and Barrytown, on a bluff overlooking the Hudson and commanding a splendid river view, dates from 1794, when Henry G. Livingston built it and sold it almost immediately to his cousin, Philip H. Livingston, who called the place *Sunning Hill.* From 1828, when Philip Livingston sold Sunning Hill to his kinsman Robert Tillotson, the place passed through various ownerships until 1860 when John Livingston came into possession and renamed it Callendar House. The wings were originally of one storey and the verandah across the west front dates from about 1830. Other minor changes have occurred from time to time, but structurally the house is little different from when it was built. The present owners are Mr. and Mrs. William H. Osborn.

MAIZEFIELD (Plate 85), built about the beginning of the 19th century, stands on a side street in Red Hook, facing the High School east of it, and is an excellent example of the large Federal Era brick house, displaying all the architectural elegancies and refinement of that period. The first recorded occupant was David Van Ness (brother of Peter Van Ness, who built Lindenwald), who served as an officer in the Continental Army during the Revolutionary War and was Brigadier-General of the Dutchess County Militia from 1793 to 1801. Jacob Van Ness (the General's son) is said to have carried Burr's challenge to Hamilton. William Van Ness, the General's nephew, was Burr's second and, according to one account, Burr went into hiding at Maizefield for a short time immediately after the duel.

General Van Ness sold Maizefield in 1815 and families of Brinckerhoffs, Tellers, Chamberlains and Timpsons lived there successively until Lawrence Timpson sold the place about 15 years ago. In the 19th century some additions were made to the south and west.

CLERMONT, TIVOLI-ON-HUDSON: WEST FRONT

PLATE 86

PLATE 87   CLERMONT, TIVOLI-ON-HUDSON: EAST OR GARDEN FRONT

COLUMBIA COUNTY

THE story of CLERMONT (Plate 86) begins with seizing a pair of legs coming down a chimney. Capture of the body belonging to the legs immediately followed in the fireplace—the captive an Indian bent on murder and robbery, the captor Robert Livingston, third son of Robert, first Lord of the Manor of Livingston.

Robert Livingston the first (came to America in 1673) was the son of the Reverend John Livingston, scion of a cadet branch of the family of the Lords Livingston of Callendar, Earls of Linlithgow. He grasped the opportunities for foresighted colonists to profit and eventually acquired a tract of 160,000 acres on the east side of the Hudson about 30 miles below Albany. In 1686 Governour Dongan created this domain the Manor of Livingston.

The marauding Indian incident explains how Clermont came to be separated from the rest of the estate and the entail to the eldest son. Robert the first sent his son Robert back to Scotland to be educated. When Robert the younger had finished his studies in Edinburgh, and afterwards read law at the Temple in London, he returned to America. Then happened the adventure Mrs. Delafield relates in her *Biographies of Francis and Morgan Lewis:*

"The first summer that young Robert passed with his father at the Manor after his return from Scotland, his attention was attracted one afternoon by what seemed to him an unusual number of Indians skulking around and keeping within the shadow of the woods. That night, after he was in bed, he heard a noise in the chimney. He lay quite still and watched; presently a pair of legs descended upon the hearth. Robert sprang from his bed, seized the fellow before he could extricate himself. . . . The man utterly confounded, confessed that he was one of a gang who had fixed upon that night to rob and murder the whites. His father was so pleased with Robert's intrepidity that he gave him the lower end of the Manor—a tract consisting of about thirteen thousand acres."

95

PLATE 88   CLERMONT, TIVOLI-ON-HUDSON: HALL AND STAIR

PLATE 89   CLERMONT, TIVOLI-ON-HUDSON: PARLOUR

This happened in the old Manor House, built in 1699, which stood on the river near the present railway station of Linlithgow. It was demolished in 1800.

At his father's death in 1728, Robert took the tract bequeathed him and, about 1730, built Clermont, a Georgian brick and stone house standing on a bluff above the Hudson. He was called "Robert of Clermont" to distinguish him from his nephew Robert, third Lord of the Manor. Robert of Clermont was a genial, courtly, picturesque figure who, till his dying day *"retained the costume of men of his rank worn at the period when he withdrew from an active part in public affairs."* His only child, the Honourable Robert R. Livingston, an *"eminent Christian, Statesman and Patriot,"* was Judge of the Admiralty Court and of the Supreme Court of the Province. In 1742 Judge Livingston married Margaret Beekman, only surviving child of Colonel Henry Beekman of Rhinebeck. She brought with her not only one of the largest estates in the

Province, but also an endowment of exceptional character, good common-sense and rare executive capacity that made her one of the most notable women of her day. She always kept abreast of what was going on, and her opinion was valued by men of public affairs. At her suggestion to a number of statesmen assembled at Clermont—just before the delegates met at Kingston to declare the Province of New York an independent State—George Clinton was chosen Governour.

At the outbreak of the Revolution, Judge Livingston removed his whole family from New York City to Clermont. Soon after this, he died; his father had died several months before. Margaret Beekman was thus left with the entire management of the vast estate; her eldest son Robert (afterwards the Chancellor) was away all the time on urgent public duty. To this task, however, Mrs. Livingston was fully equal. When General Sir John Vaughan sailed up the Hudson in October, 1777, and burned Kingston, his men fired many of the houses along

Plate 90   CLERMONT, TIVOLI-ON-HUDSON: LIBRARY
(MIRROR FROM SALOON OF THE OLD *Clermont*)

PLATE 92   THE BOUWERIE, CLERMONT VILLAGE: BEDROOM

both banks of the river. Clermont was one of the houses burned. Flames gutted the structure but left the walls standing. Undaunted by this misfortune, Margaret Livingston determined to rebuild her house despite all obstacles of war conditions. The chief difficulty was lack of skilled labour; most of the able-bodied men were either in military service or likely to be called at any moment. As a first step, she addressed the following letter to Governour Clinton:

"Claremont 19 Novr. 1778
S^r

    As you were so Obligen as to indulge me with an exemption from Military Duty for my workmen, who were Imployed in Building my farm House, I am incouraged to request the Same favor for those to be imployed in rebuilding my late Dwelling House—Many hands must Necessarily be ingaged as the House is pretty large, Such as Masons Carpenters Brick Burners Labourers & Lime Breakers and Burners—I Hope for an Exemtion for the present for My Stonebreakers & Lime Makers, who are Conrad Lasher Junr & Henry Timmerman both in Capt Tiel Rockavellers Company of the Camp—Also

for Phil Schultus under Capt Phillip Smith of the Manor as a Labourer—if y^r Excel^y will favour me my Daugh^s can bring up the Certifycate as they propose waiting upon Mrs. Clinton, to whom I beg you'll be pleased to present my Best Respects
            I am
                your Excel^{ys}
                Humble Servant
                        Marg^t. Livingston"

This letter now hangs on the wall of the living-room at Clermont.

The Governour probably remembered that he owed his post largely to Mrs. Livingston's suggestion; at any rate, she got her workmen. The materials for rebuilding were nearly all taken from the place itself. With labour commandeered from the army, Clermont soon rose from its ashes much as it was before. From ground to eaves, the rebuilding left the outside of the main body of the house nearly as it is to-day; the steep-pitched roof and the dormers, however, are alterations made about 1878. The north and south wings were added in 1800.

100

PLATE 93   THE BOUWERIE, CLERMONT VILLAGE: DINING ROOM

Before 1888 the south wing, like the north wing, was only one storey high; an upper floor was added then to give more bedrooms. About 1800—perhaps a little earlier—the present parlour and dining-room mantels were installed; also the sun-ray overdoor panels in the dining-room. The exquisite arabesque overdoor panels in the parlour were seemingly added a little later.

With Clermont rebuilt, Mrs. Livingston moved in again and continued to manage the estate; answer the many calls of charitable and relief work assumed by the women of the Revolutionary period; maintain the traditional hospitality of Clermont; oversee the education of her younger children; and superintend all the details of her large and exacting household. At Clermont negro slaves did the work in the kitchen, in the garden and on the farm. Most of them were either inherited or born on the place. While the abundance of domestic and farm labour was a great advantage, the slaves made up a large secondary family that needed unceasing supervision and instruction. They had to be looked after and thought for like children, and they imposed a great responsibility of watchful oversight and care on the white master or mistress. The slaves were kindly treated at Clermont and life went on in much the same leisurely way as on a Southern plantation. If the slaves had their allotted tasks, they had also their pleasures; festivities were regularly provided for them at certain seasons, especially Christmas. How much the slaves felt themselves a part of the place, and how content they were to be there, this incident shows. Mrs. Livingston once offered a slave woman of ungovernable temper her freedom if she would leave Clermont and never come back. The offer met an indignant refusal:

"I was born on this place and have as good a right to live here as you have. I don't want to be free."

Although he had inherited the estate at his father's death in 1775, Chancellor Livingston wished his mother to continue mistress of Clermont; this

101

PLATE 94 RICHMOND HILL, LIVINGSTON MANOR: NORTH FRONT

PLATE 95   OAK HILL, LINLITHGOW: WEST FRONT   No. 59 ON MAP

PLATE 96   LOWER VAN RENSSELAER MANOR HOUSE, CLAVERACK: SOUTH FRONT   No. 63 ON MAP

PLATE 97 THE HERMITAGE, LINLITHGOW: SOUTH FRONT

PLATE 98   CALLENDAR HOUSE, CLERMONT VILLAGE: WEST FRONT   No. 56 ON MAP

she did till her death in 1800. For himself, in 1783, he built another house, only a few hundred yards south of Clermont. The Chancellor's house, though subsequently called Arryl House, also bore the name Clermont in his time and for many years afterwards. Admiring French domestic architecture of the Neo-Classic type, he is said to have had Bunel design Arryl House on lines suggested by the Château of

Beaumarchais. Some years ago it was burned and now nothing but ruins remain. It is all a part of Clermont estate, the home of Mrs. John Henry Livingston.

THE BOUWERIE (Plate 91) near the village of Clermont, beside Roeloff Jansen's Kill, stands on land originally taken up by Major Dirck Wesselse Ten

Broeck of Albany in 1694. Some years subsequently he built a house on his land and is said to have lived there during the latter part of his life. His grandson and namesake, son of Samuel Ten Broeck and his wife, Maria Van Rensselaer, was one of the heirs to the *bouwerij;* buying the interests of the other heirs, he became sole owner and, in 1762, built what is the larger eastern or main part of the house. The older house of the early 18th century, to the west or rear, then became a subordinate feature and forms a wing of the later structure.

The name of Roeloff Jansen's Kill flowing past the house recalls an interesting bit of local history. Roeloff Jansen—the first husband of the much-married and famous Anneke Jans—was assistant *bouwmeester* or bailiff for the first Patroon Van Rensselaer. Tradition says that during an unusually severe winter in the 1630's Roeloff's boat got stuck in the ice of the Kill and he had to live with the Indians in the neighbourhood until a spring thaw released his craft so that he could go back to

Beverwyck. This *contretemps* accounted for the name of the stream.

In 1934 the Victorian verandah was removed from the east front of The Bouwerie and the house was thoroughly and painstakingly restored both outside and within. The present owner is Mrs. C. C. Townsend.

RICHMOND HILL (Plate 94), one of the many large houses on the Livingston Manor lands, is said to have been built by Walter T. Livingston, a son of Peter R. and Margaret Livingston, who lived at The Hermitage. The house bears all the architectural earmarks of the early part of the 19th century and is characterised by the generous proportions and substantial structure that marked the family ideals of building. It is also said that Walter Livingston later exchanged Richmond Hill for The Bouwerie.

OAK HILL (Plate 95) built between 1790 and 1800 by John Livingston, fifth son of the third Lord of the Manor, is about a mile and a half from the site

PLATE 101   THE HILL, HUDSON: WEST PORTICO

PLATE 102   THE HILL, HUDSON: OVAL PARLOUR

of the original Manor House of 1699 (demolished in 1800). Standing on a high bluff that rises abruptly from the river, the house commands an unparallelled outlook over long reaches of the Hudson and to the Catskills beyond. It is said that before deciding on the spot for his house, John Livingston climbed one of the tallest oak trees on the place and from that point of vantage made his decision. The rooms have very high ceilings and the site is exposed to all the north and west winds so that, while the house was a-building, the members of his family protested to the owner, *"John, you will freeze!"* It is not recorded whether their fears were realised, but the house is so soundly built that their apprehension seems needless. To a later alteration the mansard roof is due. Oak Hill is still in the possession of the family.

The LOWER VAN RENSSELAER MANOR HOUSE (Plate 96) at Claverack is said to have been built by Hendrick Van Rensselaer in 1685; it has sometimes been called the "Van Rensselaer Outpost" because it was at the lower end of the Van Rensselaer lands and conveniently placed for the transaction of manor business in that extreme part of the estate that was too far away to expect the average tenant to journey to Albany or Greenbush when rent days or court days came round. The house gradually acquired manor status with the increasing performance of manorial functions within its walls. Its early history is inseparably bound up with the history of Fort Crailo. When the Eastern Manor was set apart as a separate estate and manorial jurisdiction, the Claverack lands formed part of it, and the Claverack house became an alternative manor house for convenience in transacting manorial business. The Eastern Van Rensselaer Manor, in other words, was like a State with two capitals, Fort Crailo, the *real* Manor House, sharing its honours with Claverack.

THE HERMITAGE (Plate 97) was built with a high basement and one storey; it now has the high base-

109

PLATE 103   LUDLOW HOUSE, CLAVERACK: DOORWAY DETAIL   NO. 62 ON MAP

110

PLATE 104   LUDLOW HOUSE, CLAVERACK: SOUTH FRONT

ment and two full storeys. Just before or at the beginning of the Revolution, Colonel Peter R. Livingston, eldest son of Robert, third Lord of the Manor, was building himself a handsome brick house about 3½ miles south of the old Manor House. As he would naturally inherit the lordship of Livingston Manor, it would have been the new Manor House when he came into possession of his domain at the death of his father. When the walls had risen the height of one storey, war conditions halted further construction, had any been intended. The change of government ended the manor system and abolished the entail so that, when Robert the last Lord died, his estate and lands were divided amongst all his children instead of going to the eldest son. It is commonly said that after the war Peter Livingston then put a roof on his unfinished house of one storey and lived in it that way because of the change in his fortunes. Notwithstanding this generally-accepted story, it is not at all impossible—

111

PLATE 105 TALAVERA, CLAVERACK: WEST FRONT

PLATE 106 JACOB RUTSEN VAN RENSSELAER HOUSE, CLAVERACK:
WEST FRONT

PLATE 107   JOB CENTRE OR "OLD TURTLE" HOUSE, HUDSON: EAST FRONT   NO. 66 ON MAP

and there seems to be some architectural evidence to bear this out—that The Hermitage was never intended to have more than an exceptionally high basement, one full storey or *piano nobile* and an attic, like some of the Palladian villas or some of the plantation houses in the South, such as Gunston Hall or Mulberry Castle. Whether an upper storey was originally intended or not, the present owner of The Hermitage, Dr. Ogilvie, has added one very harmoniously. The south portico is also a modern addition.

Samuel Ten Broeck, about 1773, built CALLENDAR HOUSE (Plate 98) a mile southeast of The Bouwerie, the home of his brother, Dirck Wesselse Ten Broeck. During the Revolution Samuel Ten Broeck was a Major of Militia; after the war he became a General of Militia and also sat in the Assembly. He afterwards sold his house to Henry Livingston who gave it its present name, Callendar House.

Walter Livingston, third son of the last Lord of the Manor, married Cornelia Schuyler and, not long before the Revolution, built TEVIOTDALE (Plate 99) at Linlithgow. His daughter Harriet inherited Teviotdale and, in 1808, married Robert Fulton. Chancellor Livingston announced the engagement on the maiden trip of the *Clermont* just before the boat cast anchor for the night and landed the party of guests at Clermont. At the same time, he prophesied that the *'name of the inventor would descend to posterity as a benefactor to the world.'* Just how much the Fultons lived at Teviotdale it would be hard to say, but local tradition has always closely associated the house with the great promoter of steam navigation.

To the east of the Albany Post Road, about 4 miles south of Hudson, the white columns of a lofty portico gleam against a woodland background that crowns the hilltop. Called THE HILL (Plate 100) because of its position, the house is reminiscent of Palladio's villas on the hills about Vicenza. The original part of the house was built in 1788-89 but the complete structure, according to popularly-credited account, seems to have been finished in 1801 by an Italian architect whom the owner engaged to come here and design his countryseat. The interior also recalls Palladio; the two large oval salons, side by side, and the manner of their decoration are thoroughly Italian.

Henry Walter Livingston, for whom The Hill was built, was the eldest son of Walter Livingston of Teviotdale. Born in 1768 and graduated from Yale

114

PLATE 108 JOB CENTRE OR "OLD TURTLE" HOUSE, HUDSON: WEST FRONT

PLATE 109   JOB CENTRE OR "OLD TURTLE" HOUSE, HUDSON: SOUTH SIDE

in 1786, he began to practise law in New York City and then, in 1792, accompanied Gouverneur Morris to France as private secretary when the latter was sent as Minister Plenipotentiary. Returning to America in 1794, he continued to practise and was appointed judge of the Court of Common Pleas in Columbia County. He was twice elected to Congress and served from October 1803 to March 1807.

Henry Walter Livingston married Mary Penn Allen, granddaughter of Chief-Justice Allen of Pennsylvania. Their house was famed for graceful and profuse hospitality and amongst their guests were numerous distinguished foreigners— Louis Philippe, Joseph Bonaparte, Granville John Penn, the Marquis de la Fayette and his son, and many others. Of Joseph Bonaparte's visit Bishop Kip says:

"Thither came . . . the ex-King of Spain, who remained several days with a suite of forty persons. At the moment of his departure, when all the equipages were drawn up at the grand entrance, and Mrs. Livingston was making her adieux on the marble piazza, the princess, his daughter, called for her drawing materials. It was supposed that she wished to sketch the view, which extends for 60 miles around. But those who looked over her page discovered that it was the chatelaine she was sketching."

After Mr. Livingston's death, in 1810, Mrs. Liv-ingston continued to uphold The Hill's reputation for generous entertaining until the time of her own death in 1855. For her gracious and charming manners she was known in New York society of her day as "Lady Mary." The Hill was commonly spoken of as "Widow Mary's Place." Mr. and Mrs. E. A. Fitch now live there.

The LUDLOW HOUSE (Plate 103) in Claverack, built in 1786, is an exceptionally satisfying and convincing example of brick Georgian domestic architecture, with several conspicuous departures from the cut-and-dried sameness of interpretation that so often develops locally in one or another region. One is at a loss whether to ascribe these agreeably combined variations—such as the treatment of the gambrel roof in the composition, or the continuous arrangement of the south doorway and the Palladian window above it as a single *ensemble* of design—to partly remembered precedents in the flexible provincial Georgian interpretations in England, or to modifications and adaptations originated by local builders. In any case, the result is full of gratifying individuality. Some of the Ludlow occupants of the house are also descendants of Robert Fulton so that it has a direct association with the father of steam

PLATE 110   ABRAHAM STAATS HOUSE, STOCKPORT CREEK: SOUTH FRONT   NO. 67 ON MAP

navigation. His portrait, painted by Benjamin West, hangs in the house, along with other portraits of the Livingston and Morris relatives and connections of the Ludlows. William Henry Ludlow, who built the house, came from New York City and had extensive grain-exporting interests.

TALAVERA (Plate 105) at Claverack, was built early in the 19th century by the Honourable William W. Van Ness for his daughter who married Henry Livingston. There was much intimacy between Talavera and The Hill several miles away. Both houses stood high and in sight of each other, so there was a well-understood semaphore code between the two households by which they could send messages and get answers, day or night—a system that worked well before the day of telephones. The house is curiously but very pleasantly planned in three sections, without a central entrance; the three interior divisions are marked outside by the three western porticoes. Talavera is the home of Mr. and Mrs. J. Van Ness Philip.

The JACOB RUTSEN VAN RENSSELAER HOUSE (Plate 106) at the Red Mills, east of Claverack village,

(now the home of Mr. and Mrs. Clifford Miller), was built soon after the Revolution either on the site of, or incorporating, an earlier house built by General Robert Van Rensselaer, the father of General Jacob. The house is obviously of Georgian inspiration, but the canted corners—a most unusual feature, to say the least—and the panelled parapet suggest the dawning influence of the genial but reticent Regency or Federal Era manner that was to burst into full flower with all its lighter elegance a few years later. The mills, on the same property, have been an important factor in the life and development of the countryside since colonial times.

The JOB CENTRE OR "OLD TURTLE" HOUSE (Plate 107), on the west side of the Post Road just north of the City of Hudson, is an architectural curiosity cast in Georgian mould. The name "Old Turtle" needs no explanation; the illustrations, especially that of the south side show the fitness of the designation. It is said to have been built near the end of the 18th century by one Job Centre, and Job Centre is reputed to have been a retired ship captain. If this be the case, he apparently wished a house he could uninterruptedly circumnavigate, as one would in

117

PLATE 112   VAN ALEN ("KATRINA VAN TASSELL") HOUSE, KINDERHOOK: No. 69 ON MAP
WEST END

PLATE 113   "HOUSE OF HISTORY," KINDERHOOK: DETAIL, SOUTH FRONT   NO. 70 ON MAP

PLATE 114 "House of History," Kinderhook: South Front

PLATE 115   "House of History," Kinderhook: Hall and Stair

PLATE 116   "House of History," Kinderhook: Vista to Dining Room

taking a "constitutional" aboard ship. Both "port" and "starboard" wings have two doors, east and west, so that anyone so minded can make continuous circuits *ad libitum* around the porticoes and through the wings. The central part of the house, on the ground floor, consists of two splendid communicating rooms with semi-circular ends, east and west. Underneath the high basement is a sub-cellar (descent by a ladder—or should we say "companion-way"?) in which is a spacious wine-cellar, besides other storage room. The "Old Turtle" belongs to Mr. and Mrs. Folkers.

The ABRAHAM STAATS HOUSE (Plate 110) at the mouth of Stockport Creek (one of the places where Hendrick Hudson is said to have landed) stands on land Major Abraham Staats bought in 1654. He had come to New Netherland in 1642 as Surgeon for the West India Company. After filling this post for six years he moved to Albany, had land interests and traded with the Indians. On his land at Stockport Creek he built a house and put a farmer and his family in it. All went well until July, 1664, when the Indians burned the house with the farmer in it. The present house may be of slightly later date, or it may incorporate the walls, or at least the foundations, of the house the Indians burned. Some years ago a very old brick wing was demolished and the house has been much modernised. While it was in a half-ruinous condition a woman is said to have gone there as a bride to live, and to have lived there 40 years without ever seeing inside one of the rooms, closed because the floor had fallen in! Is there any parallel for this lack of feminine curiosity?

In a neighbourhood of old houses, LINDENWALD (Plate 111)—about 2 miles south of Kinderhook and near the Albany Post Road—is one of the most widely known through its connection with Martin Van Buren, Aaron Burr and Washington Irving. In 1780 the Honourable Peter Van Ness built a much less pretentious house on the site; this he seems to have demolished when he built the present dwelling in 1797. When the latter was first completed it was an admirable piece of late Georgian architecture characterised by all the elegancies of the late 18th century. In the Victorian era the exterior fell victim to the mania for irrelevant gables, oversized dormers and jigsaw decoration. Happily, the interior has not been spoiled and the old French polychrome landscape paper (*"Paysage à chasse"*) is still in the hall.

The Honourable William P. Van Ness succeeded his father at Lindenwald. In his law offices, in 1802, Martin Van Buren completed his preparatory legal studies. William Van Ness was Aaron Burr's inti-

mate friend and strongly supported him in the presidential campaign of 1800, when his rival, Thomas Jefferson, was elected. He was Burr's second in the fatal duel with Alexander Hamilton. Afterwards, when Burr was under the cloud of obloquy that ever hung over him, he was a frequent visitor at Van Ness's home. Indeed, Burr's ghost is said to haunt Lindenwald and one old negro manservant, years afterwards, gave a circumstantial account of meeting the apparition. The negro was going from the house to the barn when he saw, just ahead of him, a fastidiously arrayed gentleman in knee breeches whose appearance tallied exactly with that of Burr. This gentleman in knee breeches went skipping blithely along the path towards the barn, suddenly turned a series of amazing handsprings, then grew rapidly smaller and smaller, and finally disappeared from the negro's astonished gaze down a woodchuck hole. When closely questioned about his encounter, however, the darkey reluctantly owned up to having had numerous draughts of hard cyder.

Washington Irving, too, was a frequent visitor at Lindenwald. For a time, in fact, he was employed there as tutor to the children. Portions of his works were written there, and we know he drew more than one of his characters from originals in the neighbourhood, and incorporated incidents suggested to him by local happenings and current traditions.

In 1841, shortly after his defeat for re-election to the Presidency, Martin Van Buren bought Lindenwald—it was he who gave it the name—and made the place his home. It was he who made the regrettable exterior changes.

A little to the south of Kinderhook, not far from Lindenwald, is the ADAM VAN ALEN HOUSE (Plate 112), the home of one of Washington Irving's characters, "Katrina Van Tassell," in real life Katrina Van Alen. The house is an oblong one-and-a-half storey brick structure with sharply-pitched roof, built in 1737. Although in sadly dilapidated condition, it has escaped the Victorian "beautifier" who wrought such atrocities at Lindenwald. In every way the house is a good example of the 18th-century dwelling of the substantial Dutch farmers who prospered on the rich land of this countryside.

The "HOUSE OF HISTORY" (Plate 113) in Kinderhook is, before all else, a shining object lesson of what genuine appreciation and conscientious restoration of the fine things of the past can contribute to the vital enrichment of our lives to-day. Now the home of the Columbia County Historical Society, the "House of History" has regained the aspect it wore when the genius of the Federal Era or the Regency Period—call it by which name you please—inter-

preted by Barnabas Waterman of Hudson, worthily expressed the architectural ideals of an age replete with inspiration for our lasting profit.

Within its walls no events of outstanding historical moment took place; nor did its successive occupants—the Vanderpoels, the Myerses and the Burts—parade foremost in the footlights' glare of history's stage. They were decent, representative gentlefolk who graced the house they lived in and bore with dignity their share of everyday responsibilities. Whether we recall the cherry tree by the garden gate, the blooming of old-fashioned flowers, the little boys off to swim in the creek, the bride descending the stair to the candle-lighted parlour, the benign grandmother whose apron pockets held an inexhaustible store of raisins, ginger-nuts and cough-drops for her grandchildren—all these homely, intimate

incidents combine to make an *ensemble* that has the mellow quality of a still-life by one of the 17th-century Dutch masters. The house and its memories of ordered lives, the tangible and intangible together, are mysteriously blended to present the embodiment of an era.

In the course of recent ownerships, the house had suffered external injuries unthinkingly perpetrated—paint over the brickwork of the walls, irrelevant verandahs and the like. Now, its complete restoration to its original state, and its furnishing with the manner of appointments for which it was intended, have made it an eloquent exemplar for the good of all who see it and for what might be done in the rest of the Hudson Valley. An excellent library of local history and allied subjects is being collected in the house.

RENSSELAER COUNTY

THE stone house of BARENT STAATS (Plate 118) on Staats Island (once known as Papsknee or Paepsknoy) is on a farm or *bouwerij* called Hooghe Bergh (High Hill), presumably because of the knoll north of the house, on whose southern slope is the family burying ground. The building may date from one of several periods—anywhere from 1696 to 1722. Most of the evidence seems to point to the latter date. Despite its dilapidated condition, the house presents considerable architectural interest.

The VAN RENSSELAER-GENÊT HOUSE (Plate 119), on the east side of the River Road, about 3 miles north of Castleton, is an 18th-century gambrel-roofed brick structure that has suffered the usual 19th-century large-pane glazing and addition of jigsaw verandah. In its present condition it is not much to look at; it is a promising subject for restoration.

In 1742 Kiliaen Van Rensselaer, son of Hendrick, married Ariaantje Schuyler and the house is believed to have been built for the bride. Kiliaen had four sons, of whom Colonel Henry K. (born 1744) succeeded his father in possession of the house; Colonel Philip (born 1747) built Cherry Hill, across the river; Colonel Nicholas and Kiliaen were third and fourth. Colonel Henry's son Solomon was born in the house in 1774; his name also is closely associated with Cherry Hill.

Governour Clinton later bought the house. When Citizen Genêt married Cornelia Clinton instead of going home to France—as he had been told, and most of his contemporaries heartily wished he would—Governour Clinton put bride and groom in the house and sold Genêt the property in 1802. The Genêts lived there for several years until they built a larger house on the hill.

126

The house of HENDRICK BRIES (Plate 120), on the River Road about 3 miles south of Rensselaer, is believed to have been built about 1722. It is an excellent example of the late 17th and early 18th-century brick farmhouse of the region. Its steep-pitched roof, iron beam-anchors in the gable ends, and sturdy ceiling-beams supported on "knee" brackets (suggesting ship-carpentry) are thoroughly characteristic of the Dutch manner of building. The house is now in ruins.

FORT CRAILO (Plate 121), at Greenbush—now Rensselaer—opposite Albany, is one of the earliest Van Rensselaer homes in America. Its history forms part and parcel of the story of the Patroonship and Manor of Rensselaerwyck, of which it was a part until the Eastern and Western Manors were separated. In 1704, when the whole of the Van Rensselaer estate in America was finally settled after paying off the other heirs who remained in Holland, the Patroon gave his younger brother Hendrick, as his share, Fort Crailo and the Eastern Manor. From Hendrick, Fort Crailo descended to his son, Colonel Johannes, a man prominent in colonial times for his public services and patriotism. Colonel Johannes was born in the house in 1708 and lived there till his death in 1783.

Of the house we are told

"the small stone fort on the east side of the Hudson, . . . was built by order of the first Patroon. . . . It served as a place of defence and refuge for his colonists when hard-pressed by the hostile Mohicans."

The walls are brick, not stone (although on a stone foundation); the loopholes are plain evidence of defense purposes. As a matter of fact, the Rensselaerwyck colonists had little need of fort protection. Thanks to the wisdom, fairness and tact of the Directors, the colony's Indian relations were generally amicable, but when

"the Indians attacked Wiltwyck [now Kingston] and massacred many of the inhabitants, on the 17th of June, 1663, 'the farmers fled to the Patroon's new Fort Crailo at Greenbush for protection.' "

The original part of the house is said to have been built in 1642, and on a stone in its cellar wall is the inscription "K.V.R. 1642 ANNO DOMINI." On a similar stone in another wall is the inscription "DO. MEGAPOLENSIS." Though some insist the house was built in 1642, others maintain it was built a few years later and that the dated and inscribed cellar stones came from an earlier structure it superseded. In any case, Fort Crailo is a very early building and unquestionably of the 17th century. It was

both house and fort at the beginning and was named Crailo (meaning "Crows' Wood") after the estate of Crailo in Holland, which Kiliaen Van Rensselaer had bought in 1628. Whether Dominie Megapolensis occupied Fort Crailo immediately upon its completion, or whether the young Patroon's guardians leased it to *"Arendt Van Corlaer for six successive years"* (as one document indicates) is uncertain. Reverend Nicholas Van Rensselaer, the "Prophet," and his wife Alida Schuyler occupied the house and, after Nicholas died and the first Robert Livingston married the widow, the Livingstons are said to have let it to a tenant. There is a tradition that when Nicholas lay dying, Robert Livingston (often an adviser to the Van Rensselaers) appeared in the room. Nicholas, despite waning strength, sat upright and pointing at Robert shouted, *"Take that man away! He's only waiting for me to die, to*

marry my wife." Beyond question we know the Van Rensselaers occupied Fort Crailo from 1704 onwards.

In 1740 Colonel Johannes made substantial additions and brought the house to its present form. These additions comprised the cross-hall and dining-room with the rooms above, and all the rest of the L extension behind the original main structure. Large inscribed bricks, at each side of the north door, bear respectively the initials J.V.R. and the date 1740. Tradition says Fort Crailo sustained several Indian attacks prior to the Revolutionary War.

"Beautiful Katrina," Colonel Johannes's daughter, married General Philip Schuyler; their daughter Betsy became the wife of Alexander Hamilton. There was constant intercourse between Fort Crailo and The Pastures, as well as between Fort Crailo

FORT CRAILO, RENSSELAER: PARLOUR

PLATE 122

FORT CRAILO, RENSSELAER: COUNCIL CHAMBER

PLATE 123

131

and the old Manor House in Albany, and its successor. Colonel Johannes willed Fort Crailo to his grandson, John Jeremias, who made sundry alterations in the early part of the 19th century. These, however, disappeared when the house was restored.

In Fort Crailo's back garden is an old well, associated with the writing of "Yankee Doodle." During the French and Indian War, when General Abercrombie made Fort Crailo his headquarters *en route* to Ticonderoga, the officers were guests of Colonel Johannes and his wife, Angelica Livingston. On Abercrombie's staff, so the story goes, was a young surgeon, greatly amused by the spectacle the raw recruits presented as they straggled in from the countryside, arrayed in all manner of motley garb, thoroughly rustic and not at all military. Sitting on the well-kerb, he scribbled the doggerel verses which alone preserve his name and *"were destined to be adopted and proudly sung by the boys of '76."* His name is variously stated to have

been Shuckbergh, Shackberg and Stackpole; the first is generally accepted. This origin of "Yankee Doodle," it is only fair to say, is open to serious question.

In June, 1775, the Continental Army, then on its way to Ticonderoga, had its cantonment in the fields behind Fort Crailo. General Philip Schuyler also made Fort Crailo his headquarters on one occasion during the Revolution. The hospitality of the master and mistress of Fort Crailo was proverbial. Nearly all the American and French officers of note who came in the neighbourhood dined or supped there, including General Washington and the Marquis de la Fayette. In later times, Daniel Webster and Harrison Gray Otis were amongst the noted visitors. The Van Rensselaers continued to live in the house until the death of Dr. Jeremias in 1871; after that, it gradually fell into sorry decay until its restoration, on becoming State property.

SARATOGA AND ALBANY COUNTIES

THE FLATTS (Plate 125) on the river front at Watervliet, just on the northern outskirts of Albany, though part of it was probably built by the Van Rensselaers as early as 1654 and repaired or rebuilt by them in 1668, became a Schuyler house in 1672, when Philip Pieterse Schuyler bought the *bouwerij* on the river front, and it so remained until very recent years.

From Philip Pieterse The Flatts descended to his son Pieter Philipse, that picturesque and sterling personage the Indians called "Quider," whom they both feared and loved because of his just dealing and integrity. Once, partly to impress the Six Nations with England's power and partly to arouse British interest in the provincial struggle with France, "Quider" took four Mohawk chiefs to London and had the Earl of Shrewsbury present them to Queen Anne as "Kings." After that they were driven through the streets in royal carriages.

From "Quider" The Flatts passed to his son, Colonel Philip Pieterse, who married his cousin, Margarita Schuyler. This lady, commonly known in her day as "Madame Schuyler" or "Aunt Schuyler," was the subject of *Memoirs of an American Lady* by Anne McVickar Grant (published in London, 1809, and reprinted several times since in America), a valuable source for Albany's social history and manner of life just after the middle of the 18th century.

Colonel Schuyler died in 1758, and not long afterwards The Flatts caught fire and the flames destroyed the roof and interior. It was one warm summer day and Madame Schuyler was sitting in the driveway under the shade of an avenue of cherry trees. General John Bradstreet, who commanded the British troops stationed in Albany, came riding down the road to call and was startled to see smoke pouring from the top of the house. The General's fire-alarm did not in the least ruffle Madame Schuyler's composure. She calmly kept her seat under the cherry trees and from there directed the fire-fighting and the saving of such household gear as could be got out. General Bradstreet detailed some of his soldiers as workmen and, before winter, Madame Schuyler got the wing of her house rebuilt. The main part of The Flatts, facing the river, was rebuilt in its present form a little later.

As long as the Schuylers lived there, the hospitality of The Flatts was proverbial and, from the family's long and close association with Indian affairs, the hospitality often embraced deputations and visiting bands of red men. For a long time the place has been in the hands of tenants and, what with conditions usually attending farm-tenancy and the addition of some Victorian irrelevancies, the house has lost much of its rightful character—by no means, however, beyond the possibility of full restoration.

A visit to THE PASTURES (Plate 127) at Albany, the Marquis de Chastellux records in his *Travels in North America*.

"A handsome house half-way up the bank, opposite the ferry seems to attract attention and to invite strangers to stop at General Schuyler's. . . . I had recommendations to him. . . . I had besides given the rendezvous to Colonel Hamilton, who had just married another of his daughters, and who was preceded by the Vicomte de Noailles, and the Comte de Damas, who I knew were arrived the night before. The sole difficulty . . . consisted in passing the river. Whilst the boat was making its way with difficulty through the flakes of ice. . . . Mr. Lynch, who is not indifferent about a good dinner . . . mournfully says to me: 'I am sure the Vicomte and Damas are now at table, where they have good cheer and good company' . . . I diverted myself by assuring him that they saw us . . . that I even distinguished the Vicomte de Noailles who was looking at us through a telescope. . . . Never was conjecture more just. The first person we saw on shore was the Chevalier de Mauduit who was waiting for us with the General's sledge, into which we quickly stepped, and were conveyed in an instant into a handsome salon near a good fire, with Mr. Schuyler, his wife and daughters. Whilst we were warming ourselves, dinner was served, to which every one did honour, as well as to the Madeira which was excellent, and made us completely forget the rigour of the season and the fatigue of the journey."

If the Marquis does not convey an adequate architectural description of The Pastures, his vivid impression of arrival there on a cold winter's afternoon does afford a convincing sense of the homelike, hospitable atmosphere that pervaded the stately Albany house.

In February, 1761, Philip Schuyler, then twenty-eight, sailed for England; part of his errand was to adjust with the Government General Bradstreet's accounts, still unpaid after several years' standing. Although Bradstreet was a much older man, he and Schuyler were close friends. While Schuyler was getting the General's unpaid military accounts settled, Bradstreet—with Schuyler's power-of-attorney to manage his property—supervised the building of The Pastures. Work began soon after Schuyler sailed; when he returned in 1762, his new house was the first thing he saw as he neared Albany.

The Pastures is one of the finest examples of American Georgian architecture to be found anywhere. The exterior hexagonal vestibule is an addition of the late 18th century. On the upper floor, the great gallery, 20 feet wide and running the full depth of the house, was an admirable place for balls and other functions—for which it was doubtless

planned. We may well believe The Pastures quite equalled the best houses of similar character in England in the quality of its appointments, and such of the original household effects as are still preserved there confirm this opinion. Round about were gardens and orchards, vineyards and well-kept borders full of flowers, with ample expanses of lawn. Behind the house were the negro slaves' quarters—comfortable brick structures where the servants were well housed.

Philip Schuyler was fourth in descent from Philip Pieterse Schuyler, who came to Albany from Holland before 1650. When Philip was only eight, the death of his father, Johannes Schuyler, Jr., Mayor of Albany and Indian Commissioner, left him with an elder sister and two little brothers to the sole care of their mother, Cornelia Van Cortlandt Schuyler, a woman of remarkable character, highly esteemed by all. Philip was educated at home until he was about fifteen, when he was sent to school at New Rochelle. When he came of age, disregarding his rights of primogeniture, he made an equal division of the estate with his brothers and sister.

At the outbreak of the French and Indian War, he raised a company and was commissioned Captain by James De Lancey, then Governour of the Province. In 1768, along with Jacob Ten Eyck, he sat for the City and County of Albany in the Provincial Assembly. Thence onward he stoutly espoused the side of the Colonies against the measures of the British Government; some of the boldest resolutions of the Assembly he draughted, and at his suggestion Edmund Burke was appointed Agent for New York in England. In 1775 he was a member of the Continental Congress; Major-General of the Northern Department under Washington from 1775 to 1777; a second time member of the Continental Congress in 1779; and, with Rufus King, one of the first two United States Senators from New York. He further served his State as Surveyor-General, Chairman of the Board of Indian Commissioners, and one of the Commissioners to settle the Massachusetts and Pennsylvania boundaries disputes. No less useful and unselfish in private life, always in the forefront of any undertaking that might benefit community or State, he was conspicuous for his integrity, kindliness of heart and manner, generosity, affability, courtliness, as became a gentleman of the old school, and his unfailing hospitality, not only to the numerous distinguished friends who frequented his house, but also the many of lesser note who chanced to come thither. Such was the master of The Pastures.

Its mistress was the *Sweet Kitty V.R.* of Schuyler's youthful letters, daughter of Johannes Van

Rensselaer of Fort Crailo, just across the river. Lossing describes her as strikingly beautiful. Besides beauty, Mrs. Schuyler had determination and firmness of will, executive ability and, as a grace to her other qualities, spontaneous kindness of heart and action. She displayed fortitude in the face of danger, and also quick judgment and initiative when crises arose, as they did more than once in the course of her life. Perhaps the incident by which her daring and independence are best remembered was her hurried visit to Schuylerville, as Burgoyne's army was approaching from the north. The panic-stricken refugees fleeing towards Albany were amazed to see a carriage with a single armed escort hastening north. Mrs. Schuyler sat composedly within. She was bound toward Saratoga to fetch away her household treasures from her summer home at Schuylerville. When the fugitives protested against her continuing, she merely smiled and said, *"The General's wife mustn't be afraid,"* and kept right on undaunted. When she had rescued such valuables as she could carry with her, she set fire with her own hands to the grain fields and then drove back to Albany. General Burgoyne occupied the house just before the Battle of Saratoga, and then burned it as a military measure. General Schuyler afterwards rebuilt the house, as seen in the illustration (Plate 126). There is a tradition that straightway after the battle the General engaged enough artisans from the victorious American army to finish the rebuilding in 17 days! The house may not have been rebuilt, however, till 1783.

After the Battle of Saratoga, General Schuyler's treatment of Baron and Baroness Riedesel and other captives was chivalrously considerate. Following the surrender, when General Schuyler met General Burgoyne, what took place is best told in Burgoyne's own words in a speech before the House of Commons:

"I expressed to General Schuyler my regret at the event which had happened [the burning of Schuyler's Schuylerville house], and the reasons which had occasioned it. He desired me to think no more of it, saying that the reason justified it according to the rules of war. . . .

He did more: he sent his aide-de-camp to conduct me to Albany, in order, as he expressed it, to procure me better quarters than a stranger might be able to find. This gentleman conducted me to a very elegant house and, to my great surprise, presented me to Mrs. Schuyler and her family; and in General Schuyler's house I remained during my whole stay at Albany, with a table of more than twenty covers for me and my friends, and every other possible demonstration of hospitality."

It was in the southeast parlour at The Pastures that the marriage of Elizabeth Schuyler and Alexander Hamilton took place in December, 1780. This wedding was, perhaps, the most brilliant and festive assemblage the house was ever to witness. "Betsy" was the only one of the General's daughters to marry with his previous consent. Instead of leaping from a window and eloping with the man of her choice, seeking parental sanction and forgiveness after marriage as a *fait accompli,* she was wed in the orthodox manner. Her wedding was as joyous and splendid an affair as parental affection, wealth, a wide family connection and innumerable friends could make it. It was a happy marriage, and from then till the end of his life Hamilton was a frequent sojourner at The Pastures.

During 1781, the "Cowboys"—those worthless scalawags who claimed to be Loyalists but were merely lawless hooligans bent on violence and robbery, and a disgrace to the allegiance they professed —with Canadian and Indian confederates were making every effort to kidnap prominent citizens of Albany and carry them off to Canada to hold for ransom. General Schuyler, of course, was the chief quarry. Warned of their intentions and knowing that figures had been seen skulking in the shrubbery, the General *"kept a guard of six men constantly on duty, three by day and three by night."* He and his family were on the alert. The attack came towards evening of a sultry August day. The story of Margaret Schuyler's dash up the stair with her sister's baby in her arms; the tomahawk hurled at her by the Indian, that missed its mark and stuck in the handrail; and the panic flight of the ruffians with stolen silver and captive guards, every reader knows. When the guards were afterwards exchanged as prisoners of war and found their way back to Albany, General Schuyler gave each of them a farm in Saratoga County.

The Pastures is now the property of the State and maintained as an historic monument.

When the second VAN RENSSELAER MANOR HOUSE (Plate 132) was threatened some years ago with impending demolition, it was carefully taken down, removed to Williamstown, Massachusetts, and the main portion re-erected there. It is occupied by the Sigma Phi Society and preserved as a valued historical and architectural monument.

The Jonkheer Kiliaen Van Rensselaer, a nobleman of the Province of Guelderland, was one of the original "Lords Directors" of the Dutch West India Company, likewise one of the Amsterdam Chamber in the Assembly of the XIX. Moved by the spirit of enterprise and adventure, he notified his colleagues of his intentions to become a Patroon under the "Charter of Freedoms and Exemptions." Accordingly, he sent his agents to New Netherland to choose for him land for the planting of a "colonie." Between April and mid-August, 1630, he procured to be purchased for him from the Indian proprietors several large tracts of land on both the east and west banks of the Hudson so that when patents from Director Pieter Minuit and the Council at Manhattan

PLATE 127 THE PASTURES, ALBANY: EAST FRONT

PLATE 128   THE PASTURES, ALBANY: WEST SIDE

PLATE 129   THE PASTURES, ALBANY: THE LONG GALLERY

PLATE 130   THE PASTURES, ALBANY: NORTH PARLOUR

confirmed these purchases, a great portion of the present counties of Albany and Rensselaer was in the hands of the Patroon and Fort Orange, with the land immediately around its walls, was all that remained in the neighbourhood under the sole jurisdiction of the West India Company.

The stable foundation and substantial success of the Van Rensselaer Patroonship as a venture in colonisation and concentrated local government were altogether due to just one person, Kiliaen Van Rensselaer, the first Patroon. He never had the gratification of seeing his vast overseas domain, yet he laboured so assiduously, so wisely and so well that no one of the early pioneers actually on the ground, combatting face to face the dangers and hardships of subduing the wilderness, is more to be reckoned a founder and maker of the country. They toiled with their hands and sweated, and in their bodies endured the physical discomforts incident to early settlement; they had also the satisfaction of seeing the tangible results of their effort and sacrifice. Van

Rensselaer sat in his counting-house in Amsterdam, planned with painful anxiety, devised ways and means to meet the endless needs of a venture that entailed an enormous outlay and brought in little return; directed with meticulous care every detail of his distant undertaking; and showed his faith by unflinching devotion to the furtherance of a scheme that he must well have known could never be of profit to himself personally and could bear fruit only for succeeding generations. And Van Rensselaer's only meed of satisfaction came from the reports of his agents which, often enough, were insufficient, perplexing and far from encouraging. Yet Van Rensselaer toiled on unremittingly. Although an absentee landlord, he deserves none of the odium usually attaching to that class, and for what he did he richly merits the honour and gratitude of posterity.

Examination of documents relating to the intimate affairs of the colony in its early days discloses enough incidents to convey a lively impression of what was going on in the everyday routine of building the settlement. For instance, in July, 1631,

> "appeared before the meeting [of the Amsterdam Chamber of the West India Company] Mr. Kiliaen Van Rensselaer, who requested that he be permitted to send over by the ship *d'Eendracht* some colonists and eight or ten calves." An ensuing entry reads: "In regard to which it was decided first to hear the skipper, who declares that he will do all he can, whereupon his honour's request is granted, on condition that the skipper in case he should be inconvenienced thereby, may throw them overboard or allow them to be eaten, without thereby obliging the Company to give any compensation."

Although the record does not specifically say so, it is to be presumed the discretionary powers given the skipper to throw overboard or eat part of the Patroon's shipment, should he *be inconvenienced thereby,*" referred to the calves, not the colonists—although one cannot help wondering whether, in the course of a long sea voyage, it might not at times have been a satisfaction to the skipper had the option of disposal been all-inclusive. The minute directions Van Rensselaer sent his agents are full of homely details that bring the daily life of the settlers very close to us. In case the agents

> "think it advisable to erect a brandy distillery or brewery, they shall ask the director [of the Company] for the large brewing kettle and brandy kettle which is at the Manhattes or elsewhere."

With well-balanced judgment and sympathetic comprehension of the divers needs of humanity, while taking thought for the *spirituous* comfort—an indicated by the memorandum just quoted—the Patroon concerned himself with the no less necessary *spiritual* comfort of his people, for he enjoins Commissary Planck

> "before all things to promote piety and take care that means be found to send a minister," and instructs Pieter Cornelissen that he shall, meanwhile, "cause the people to assemble every Sunday, to train them in the commandments, the psalms, the reading of the Holy Scriptures and Christian authors, in modesty, love and decency."

This happy combination of brewing and preaching, the inculcation of piety and the distilling of brandy, plainly show the Patroon's catholic outlook and his fitness to be at the head of a colonisation venture in which human nature was bound to play a major part. Rum and decency are more naturally allies than rum and damnation.

The first Manor House, built in Albany about 1660, was the centre of much of the earlier history of the Patroonship and Manor, as well as of much of the family history. There were several thousand tenants on the Manor and on rent days, and the days when the Manor Courts were held, there were notable gatherings of the tenantry. The old Manor House was not only the home of the Patroons and the seat of the local manorial government, but it was also used as a fort in the earlier days of the colony. When the family moved to the new Manor House nearby, completed by Stephen Van Rensselaer in 1765, the old house was relegated to other uses. The new Manor House, a stately Georgian structure designed with the utmost elegance characteristic of the period, was far more in keeping than was its predecessor with the station of its owners, and far better suited to the lavish and constant hospitality dispensed. The great central block was flanked by one-storey wings, and all the amenities of orders, balustrades and balconies, besides a wealth of subsidiary details, graced the exterior. So long as the Van Rensselaer family lived in this house, the guests welcomed within its doors were the most notable personages who came to Albany, and the functions held there brought the presence of many whose names are familiar in the annals of the country.

Colonel Philip Van Rensselaer (son of Colonel Kiliaen and Ariaantje Schuyler Van Rensselaer), who was born in the Van Rensselaer-Genêt house on the opposite side of the river, built CHERRY HILL (Plate 133) at the time of his marriage (1768) to Marie Sanders, a granddaughter of Peter Schuyler. Philip's daughter Arriet married her cousin Solomon Van Rensselaer (son of her father's brother Henry). After Colonel Philip's death, his son-in-law Solomon bought Cherry Hill and his half-century of occupancy gave the house a considerable share of traditional interest.

Before he was eighteen, Solomon Van Rensselaer began his military career under General Anthony Wayne. Wounded in the battle of the Miami, he served in the Niagara frontier campaign and was again wounded in the Battle of Queenstown. Later, he was Adjutant-General of New York State, Postmaster of Albany, and a member of Congress. In 1824, when the Marquis de la Fayette visited Albany, General Van Rensselaer was his host and entertained him at Cherry Hill. From General Van Rensselaer, Cherry Hill passed by several inheritances to its present owner and occupant, Mrs. Edward W. Rankin. Occupied by one family for nearly two centuries, Cherry Hill has escaped mutilations and preserved the quality and characteristics that only an uninterrupted succession in family ownership can impart.

The HENDRICK VAN WIE HOUSE (Plate 135), built in 1732, is one of the most interesting brick farmhouses in the whole region. The walls bear Van Wie's initials and the date. Near the river, the house is about 4 miles below Albany and faces east; its site on the southern slope of a hill necessitates an high basement (quite above ground at the south end) and a flight of steps to the door on the main floor. The brickwork is excellent, but especially

PLATE 131   THE PASTURES, ALBANY: SOUTH PARLOUR

noteworthy are the brick-cheeked dormers with chimney-like brick finials and the dormer peaks, above the window openings, nogged with brick-work. There are little granary-doors high in one gable end. Unfortunately the house is falling to ruin. It is not, however, beyond possibility of repair.

In 1736, Rensselaer Nicoll—great grand-nephew of Colonel Richard Nicoll, first Governour of the Province of New York—built the first part of BETH-LEHEM HOUSE (Plate 136), just south of Vlauman's Kill, a few miles below Albany. Its face towards the river, Bethlehem House is a brick structure of four successive stages of growth—its 1736 body was extended to the south in 1795; in 1812, the 1795 part received an addition to the west; and, in 1820, the original 1736 portion had also a western addition. Francis, the son of Rensselaer Nicoll, inherited

Bethlehem House and from him it descended to his daughter Elizabeth who married Captain Richard Sill in 1785. The Sill descendants continued to own and occupy the place and, in 1925, Dunkin H. Sill wrote for the *New York Genealogical and Biographical Record* an account of the old slave Caesar, who was born at Bethlehem and spent his entire life of 115 years there. Mr. Sill's account of Caesar incidentally gives an intimate picture of the family life and tells how they were accustomed every winter to travel by sleigh down the west side of the river to New York City, stopping on the way for days together at the homes of numerous relatives and friends; spend several weeks in the city being entertained, entertaining, and enjoying city diversions; and then sleigh back up the east side of the Hudson with a further succession of visits to their wide connection of kindred at each stage of the progress. In

Van Rensselaer Manor House, (now re-erected in Williamstown, Massachusetts)

Plate 132

PLATE 134   CHERRY HILL, ALBANY: SOUTH END FROM GARDEN

the spring, summer and autumn they were at Bethlehem House to receive and entertain those whose hospitality they had enjoyed on their winter pilgrimage.

ARIAANTJE COEYMANS'S HOUSE (Plate 137), built about 1716, is at Coeymans, in full view from the highway. Barent Pieterse Coeymans as a lad entered the service of the Patroon Van Rensselaer in 1639 and became a miller. Industrious and thrifty, by 1657 he was able to lease and operate mills himself. In 1673 he bought from the Indians a large tract of land, established mills and built himself a house where the town of Coeymans now is. He died a wealthy man some time between 1706 and 1714; his estate was divided in 1716. His house, commonly called "Coeymans's Castle," was subsequently demolished.

His daughter Ariaantje (born in 1672) was a mature spinster when her father died and had presumably led a repressed and narrow life, contrary to her inclinations. When she came into her inheritance in 1716 she was forty-four years old. She built herself a large, handsome house that outstripped any others of its day in the neighbourhood in point of size and elegance; had her full-length portrait painted; and, in 1723, when she was fifty-one, married a husband of twenty-eight. The wedding took place in her new house. As might have been expected, the marriage proved unhappy. She died in 1743 at the age of seventy-one—it is generally believed, a lonely and disappointed woman. Her wealth came too late for her to enjoy it as she had hoped. Her house seems the monument of a frustrated life. It originally had a gabled roof and the walls at the gable-ends were crow-stepped. The gambrel roof dates from the latter part of the 18th century. Italian tenants now occupy the house.

144

PLATE 135   HENDRICK VAN WIE HOUSE, BELOW ALBANY: EAST FRONT   NO. 79 ON MAP

PLATE 136   BETHLEHEM HOUSE, CEDAR HILL: EAST FRONT   NO. 80 ON MAP

146

PLATE 137　　　　　ARIAANTJE COEYMANS'S HOUSE, COEYMANS: GENERAL VIEW　　　NO. 81 ON MAP
FROM HIGHWAY

PLATE 138 PIETER BRONCK HOUSE, WEST COXSACKIE: 1663 PART (LEFT)
AND "NEW HOUSE," 1738 (RIGHT)

GREENE COUNTY

THE PIETER BRONCK HOUSE (Plate 138), at West Coxsackie, is one of the outstanding and exceptionally illuminating architectural monuments of the State, for it is thoroughly representative of the 17th and 18th-century Dutch manner of building in the upper Hudson Valley. Furthermore, it has never been spoiled by the damaging alterations and disfigurements that befell so many Hudson River houses of its own or later date—disfigurements that were perpetrated especially during the Victorian era when the unrestrained mania for romantic "prettyfying" let loose a horde of fretted bargeboards, jigsaw-decorated verandahs, misplaced gables and uninspired mansard roofs, "planted" on defenceless bodies to which they were utterly alien. Such minor changes as were made to the fabric of the Pieter Bronck house were so slight and superficial that "restoration" was almost too simple and easy a matter to be dignified by that impressive term. Having preserved intact the typical characteristics and details of local domestic architecture of the days when the several parts of the house were built, it is an invaluable architectural and historical document.

Jonas Bronck, who came to New Amsterdam in 1639 with his family and servants, was a Dane of apparently substantial means and good education. The small library he is said to have brought with him was exceptional for colonists of that period. The land he bought and settled to the north of Manhattan—the present Bronx—took its name from him. After his death, in 1643, his widow married Arendt Van Corlaer (a relative of the Van Rensselaers) and went to live in Rensselaerwyck, taking her young son, Pieter Bronck, with her. It is not unlikely that the Van Corlaers may have lived for a time in Fort Crailo; a document implying that they did has already been mentioned.

When Pieter Bronck, who appears to have been a thrifty and energetic lad, grew up, he conducted a brewery in Beverwyck. In 1661 he mortgaged his brewery and, in 1662, bought from the Indians a tract of land near the present West Coxsackie. In 1662 or 1663, according to the understanding at the

148

PLATE 139   PIETER BRONCK HOUSE, WEST COXSACKIE: EAST FRONT OF GROUP   No. 82 ON MAP

PLATE 140   PIETER BRONCK HOUSE, WEST COXSACKIE:
1663 BODY WITH 1792 ADDITION

PLATE 141   PIETER BRONCK HOUSE, WEST COXSACKIE: DETAIL, GABLE END
OF "NEW HOUSE," 1738

PLATE 142   PIETER BRONCK HOUSE, WEST COXSACKIE:
                                    LIVING ROOM, "NEW HOUSE," 1738

PLATE 143
PIETER BRONCK HOUSE, WEST COXSACKIE:
LIVING ROOM IN 1663 PART

time of purchase that he would straightway settle upon his land, he went there to live and develop his holding. In 1663 he reared the oldest part of the house. It was staunchly built with thick walls of native stone and consisted of one large room on the ground floor, with another room above it and a lofty attic above that. All the joists are tremendously heavy beams and the floor boards are 15 inches or more in width. The stair, in one corner of the ground floor room, is like a ship's companionway. The windows have small-paned casements and unusually heavy panelled shutters, and the attic is lighted by two brick-faced obliquely-set bull's-eye windows, about the size of portholes, in each gable end. The roof is of very steep pitch and high.

Pieter Bronck died in 1669. His family prospered and, in 1738, a much-needed enlargement of the original dwelling came in the form of a brick addition—really a separate structure called "the New House," connected with the older stone building by a covered brick passage that is actually a hall. The "New House" has two rooms on the ground floor, two above and, again, a capacious attic in the steep and high roof. The method of supporting the ends of the heavy joist beams on "knee" brackets (Plate 142) is suggestive of ship-carpentry. This feature occurs in a number of Dutch farmhouses of about the same period, on both sides of the upper Hudson. As may be seen from Plate 141, the brickwork of the "New House" is of beautiful quality, its colour a warm orangey salmon pink. The small shuttered opening in the upper part of the gable-end is a granary door. An uncommon and interesting item is to be seen in the brick cheeks of the dormers.

In 1792 the family enlarged the stone building of 1663 by adding to its west side a hall and a dining-room (Plate 144), with attic above. Although the construction by that time had become generally

153

PLATE 144   PIETER BRONCK HOUSE, WEST COXSACKIE: DINING ROOM,
1792 ADDITION TO 1663 PART

much lighter, this addition nevertheless exhibits the same massive methods used in the older parts of the house. The panelling of the west or fireplace wall in the 1792 dining-room is especially beautiful; indeed, the woodwork throughout all parts of the house is exceptionally good.

Lands and house passed by inheritance from one generation to another and remained in the family until the house with the plot of ground on which it stands came as a memorial into the care of the Greene County Historical Society. It was never the scene of any events of conspicuous historical import but, thanks to the conservative inclinations of the family—who were always representative of the best substantial element that formed the backbone of the country from early colonial times onward—the whole fabric has been preserved in a state of perfection rarely equalled in a building of its age. There is not a feature or detail in any part of the structure that will not repay careful study and provide a mass

of profitable suggestion. The Pieter Bronck House is furnished throughout and is kept open to the public by the Greene County Historical Society which makes its headquarters there.

The JAN VAN LOON HOUSE (Plate 145) at Athens, was built in 1706 by Jan Van Loon, who came to this country from Holland about 1686. The extensive Loonenburg Patent, in what is now Greene County, took its name from Jan Van Loon, who was one of the chief patentees of the broad lands included in that grant. From this hardy pioneer progenitor, who dwelt in this small but sturdily built house (now indicated by a roadside marker) while he was taming the wilderness and laying the foundations of future well-being for his family, have sprung numerous descendants who have in their several generations justified the vision and enterprise of their forebear. In 1720 Jan Van Loon is said to have divided his lands amongst his sons. To the

PLATE 145   JAN VAN LOON HOUSE, ATHENS: VIEW FROM NORTHEAST   NO. 83 ON MAP

eldest son, Matthias, eventually descended this house in Athens near the shore of the Hudson.

The EUGENE VAN LOON HOUSE (Plate 146) at Athens, known also as the Gantley House, stands on a knoll overlooking the little Jan Van Loon house a few hundred feet down the slope, and commanding a wide view up and down the Hudson and over the opposite shores. According to local tradition, the house was being planned just before the War of 1812. The mistress of the house-to-be was set upon having an oval ball room. The master couldn't see the point of any such folly, said he didn't wish an oval ball room and wouldn't have it. He went away to the war and his spouse superintended the building of the house. When the head (?) of the family came home after the war, his house was finished, and there was the oval ball room (Plate 148)! If this tale isn't true, it ought to be. The reader is left to draw the moral. Barnabas Waterman, of Hudson, who designed the "House of History" in Kinderhook, was also the architect for this house. Exquisite detail, from the unusual recessed doorway of the east front (Plate 147), to the least item of interior

finish, bears witness to the scholarship and discriminating taste of an architect who deserves to be better known and remembered for his work in the Hudson Valley.

The VAN VECHTEN HOUSE (Plate 149), at Catskill, stands back from a side road, some distance northwest of Catskill town. A nearby roadside historical marker acquaints the seeker of old houses that here, at Mawignack, Dirck Teunisse Van Vechten built his house in 1690; that there was an Indian fort on the hill to the north; and that there was a footpath leading to a ford, to the east. The house is built on the brow of a wooded declivity that falls abruptly down to the Catskill Creek on the south. As early as 1660, the low lands between the foot of the sharp descent and the banks of the creek appear to have been leased to one Van Bremen, who built a stone house there. This was destroyed by a freshet. Whether he built another house at the top of the hill, and the present house is partly on those foundations, is not known. At any rate, Dirck Teunisse Van Vechten bought the land in 1681 and, save for a 40-years' interval between 1832 and 1872, the prop-

PLATE 146   EUGENE VAN LOON (GANTLEY) HOUSE, ATHENS: EAST FRONT   NO. 84 ON MAP

PLATE 147   EUGENE VAN LOON (GANTLEY) HOUSE, ATHENS: DOORWAY

PLATE 148   EUGENE VAN LOON (GANTLEY) HOUSE, ATHENS: OVAL BALL ROOM

PLATE 149   VAN VECHTEN HOUSE, CATSKILL: NORTH FRONT   No. 85 ON MAP

PLATE 150   DU BOIS HOUSE, CATSKILL: C. 1750 BUILDING AND
END OF C. 1803 ADDITION

erty has always remained in the Van Vechten family.

In just what house, or what kind of house, Dirck Teunisse and his family lived, between 1681 and 1690, is not clear, but the tradition is very definite in the Van Vechten family that the oldest part of the present house was built in 1690. Although the house has undergone so many alterations and additions in the course of years that it is well-nigh impossible to tell exactly what it was like originally, it has nevertheless preserved a distinct individuality representative of the colonial period and endless features of remarkable interest, from door latches and pulls to excellent and rather unusual panelling in different rooms. Incidentally, it affords a good example of the now rare bed-recess or "bed-sink" that could be closed in by sliding panels.

The exterior has been a good deal modernised, but the interior is in great measure unspoiled. In her *Catskill of the Yesterdays,* Mrs. Jessie V. V. Vedder, the Greene County Historian, has made a vehicle of the Van Vechten house and its occupants for an illuminating picture of life and manners in Greene County during the whole colonial period.

In the town of Catskill, the DU BOIS HOUSE (Plate 150) enjoys the rare distinction of being one of those dwellings made by the joining of two separate structures wholly different in date and in style, where the older part has been allowed to retain all its characteristics without any attempt to bring it into conformity with the later part, or even to remedy what many people of the present day would undoubtedly consider its shortcomings. Each part, according to its own proper genius, has been made the most of. The small original stone house (c. 1750), built in the rugged simplicity of the local Dutch manner, faces south, looks out toward the drive and the gardens, and contains the dining-room and kitchen, on the ground floor, with bedrooms above. The 1803-4 stuccoed part (much larger), fronting east directly on the road, with the creek parallelling it, exhibits in full measure all the poise, suavity and calculated refinements of the Regency or Federal manner, of which it is a successful expression. The two-tiered verandah surrounding the 1803-4 part of the house, dictated by varying ground levels, is reminiscent of Charleston and New Orleans. In the Regency parlour occurs an unusual bit of design in the fireplace and the over-mantel panel above it. Mr. and Mrs. William Palmatier now occupy the house.

159

PLATE 151

DU BOIS HOUSE, CATSKILL: EAST FRONT

No. 86 ON MAP

PLATE 152   DU BOIS HOUSE, CATSKILL: PARLOUR

ULSTER COUNTY

ULSTER COUNTY is peculiarly rich in old stone houses of thoroughly Dutch origin. Some of them date wholly or in part from the 17th century, many more from the 18th. A few have preserved their pristine character intact. The majority have undergone some degree of alteration or enlargement but, in nearly every case, the original type is clearly recognisable and complete restoration could readily be achieved. Sometimes the external damage has been limited to a jigsaw Victorian porch and large-pane glazing in the windows. Structurally they are so substantial that anything more than superficial disfigurement, either inside or out, would be really difficult.

Coming from the north along the West Shore highway, one of the first Ulster County Dutch stone houses the traveller sees is the SCHOONMAKER HOUSE (Plate 153) on the northern outskirts of Saugerties, at the junction of Main and Malden Streets. According to a date-stone in the south or front wall, the house was built in 1727 and Samuel Schoonmaker is believed to have been the builder and first

occupant. His son Egbert, who inherited the house, was a Captain in the American Army during the Revolutionary War, an Elder of the Katzbaan Church and a member of the General Committee of the Articles of Association. The property has always remained in the family. Externally the house is unchanged save for the addition of a double dormer and a Victorian verandah on the south front. At the east end is a detached stone building, of a type often found close by these houses, which may have served either for slave quarters or as a summer kitchen.

Kingston, and the country immediately round about Kingston, has a wealth of old Dutch stone houses. The town itself, despite all its modern growth, takes its true atmosphere from them, and they are a source of universal and justifiable pride to Kingstonians, whose families, for the most part, have some direct connection with one or another of these sturdy old dwellings, not a few of which date from the town's infancy. Kingston may be said to have begun life in 1653 when the first permanent

PLATE 154   "SENATE HOUSE" (TEN BROECK HOUSE), KINGSTON: EAST FRONT   NO. 88 ON MAP

PLATE 155   "SENATE HOUSE" (TEN BROECK HOUSE), KINGSTON: WEST FRONT

settlers established themselves on the fertile lands along the Esopus. At the outset, there was no attempt to found a really organised village or town. The settlers, more intent on husbandry than anything else, built their farmhouses on their lands wherever they pleased. This easy-going method of letting town-organisation take care of itself might have been well enough had it not been for the Indians. Having tasted the white man's "fire-water" and got at odds with certain of the farmers, the Indians became a menace; it was clearly necessary to take measures for self-protection. In May, 1653, the settlers sent Governour Stuyvesant a petition for help saying:

> "The savages compel the whites to plough their maize land and, when they hesitate, threaten, with firebrands in their hands, to burn their houses. . . . The chiefs have no control over their men. . . . We are locked up in our houses and dare not move a limb."

Governour Stuyvesant came with 60 or 70 armed men the day before Ascension Day and gave the people notice to meet him the next afternoon after service. He then told them plainly that

> 'the killing of one man and the burning of two buildings was not enough to make war. They must concentrate and form a village with a stockade, so as to be able to protect themselves.'

They begged the Governour to let the soldiers stay, and to let them postpone building until after harvest. To this Stuyvesant consented, if they would agree to gather in a village.

The next day he conferred with the Indian warriors and upbraided them for their insolence, murder and burnings. Still, he told them, he had not come to make war but to punish the guilty and find out why they were acting thus. After a little, one of the chiefs said:

> 'the Shawanakins sold their children drink, and were thus the cause of the Indians being made crazy, which was the cause of all the mischief. The sachems could not always control the young men, who would often fight and wound. The murder was committed not by one of their tribe, but by a Minnesink, who had skulked away among the Haverstraws. The one who fired the two small dwelling-houses had run away, and dared not cultivate his own soil. They were innocent, not actuated by malice, did not want to fight, but could not control the young men.'

The result of all these explanations was that Stuyvesant told the Indians they must repair all damages, seize the murderer if he came among them, and do no more mischief; that the Dutch were now going to live in one spot; and that they ought to sell all the Esopus lands to the Dutch and move farther into the interior, because it was not good for them to be so near the *Shawanakins, whose cattle might eat your maize, and thus cause frequent disturbances."*

The Indians acquiesced, and the Dutch signed an agreement to live in a palisaded village. A site for the town duly chosen, at the time agreed the Dutch set to work with a will to build the stockade as the Lord-Director ordered. In three weeks they completed a substantial palisade, moved the buildings, threw a bridge over the brook beyond the gate, and built a guard-house and temporary barracks. The people now felt more secure, but there were always distant rumblings of trouble with the natives and the Dutch were still not always either considerate or prudent in their relations with the red men. Their own actions, indeed, often fomented mutual distrust. In the autumn of 1659 some of them were themselves responsible for a dastardly outrage which,

> "entirely unprovoked and uncalled for, set the warwhoop resounding throughout the country, accompanied with all the horrors of savage warfare."

Being given a jug of brandy, a few Indians had a frolic and became noisy. The report that Indians were having a drunken spree was enough to set several hotheads in the town a-going. Against the orders of Ensign Smit, eight or nine of them set out and attacked the Indians, who were by then lying in a stupour,

> "firing a volley of musketry among them, killing some and wounding others. . . . The Dutch thereupon returned to the fort with great speed, after that *most valiant* exploit, murdering Indians stupidly drunk."

As was to be expected, war to the knife followed this outrage; peace was restored, only after much bloodshed and sorrow on both sides, by the treaty entered into *"under the blue sky of heaven,"* July 15, 1660.

In May 1661 the town received a charter conferring municipal powers; the name "Wiltwyck" was bestowed on it to commemorate the fact that *"the soil was a free gift from the Indians."* A schout and three schepens were to administer the government, and pay *"due attention to the conduct, conversation, and abilities of honest and decent persons."* Schout and schepens were to hold their court every fortnight, harvest-time excepted, unless necessity might otherwise require.

> "All criminals and delinquents guilty of wounding, bloodshed, fornication, adultery, public and notorious thefts, robberies, smuggling of contraband, blasphemy, violating God's holy name and religion, injuring or slandering the supreme magistrates or their representatives," were to be referred to the Director-General and Council of New Netherland. Lesser crimes, and misdemeanours, including "quarrels, injuries, scolding, kicking, beating, threatening" and the like were left to the adjudication of the local magistrates.

In spite of the paternalistic supervision enjoined to order the little town in all godliness and quietness, the *"old Adam"* was rampant in some of the villagers and would out, now and again, to the public scandal, resulting in such unseemly actions as kick-

ing and calling of names! Probably these occasional village rumpuses were a welcome and wholesome relief to the tedium of humdrum bucolic existence. Besides the fatherly oversight of manners and morals prescribed, the Director-General promulgated a set of by-laws—a naïve combination of injunctions to regulate temporal and spiritual affairs, moral behaviour and the performance of civic duties! It is diverting to learn on what days one might or might not get drunk with impunity; it is equally diverting to find obligations of Sunday sobriety in the same category of sanctions as the prohibition of wooden chimneys, while the iniquity of proposing a religious dispute stands shoulder to shoulder with the duty of keeping fences and gates in good order. From this it is evident where some of our modern law-makers look for inspiration.

The old Dutch houses with which Kingston still abounds are substantially built of the native limestone. To one not accustomed to them, these colonial Dutch dwellings are a source of wonder. As you first look at them, they seem modest-sized, low-roofed, oblong structures of sturdy masonry, with little slope-topped dormers peeking over the eaves. Most of them are one-and-a-half storey buildings; before the doors are often *stoeps* with settles at each side. But cross the threshold, and a surprise awaits you. Room after room opens out from somewhere, you can't quite imagine where. You dodge around a corner and unexpectedly find yourself in a room whose existence you could not have guessed. You open a door, thinking to find a cupboard, and behold, there is yet another room staring you in the face. Apparently the law in physics about two things occupying the same space at the same time doesn't hold good here. Then, equally surprising, there is a really good-sized upstairs, roomy enough to hold endless household gear. Now you are ready to believe the saying that a Dutchman's house is like his breeches—capable of holding anything he can cram inside.

After the reduction of Forts Montgomery and Clinton in the Highlands, during the Revolutionary War, General Sir John Vaughan came up the

PLATE 158   VAN STEENBURGH HOUSE, KINGSTON: SOUTH FRONT   No. 90 ON MAP

river to Kingston. In writing afterwards of the burning of the town, General Vaughan said:

"Esopus [Kingston was still very commonly called Esopus] being a nursery for almost every Villain in the Country, I judged it necessary to proceed to that town."

Having arrived there, he judged it necessary also to burn it, which he did, October 16, 1777. Only one house in Kingston escaped the touch of fire, and this "fireproof" house, as a local historian has dubbed it, was the VAN STEENBURGH HOUSE (Plate 158). A tablet on the front of the house commemorates the burning of the town and this single instance of immunity from the flames, but it does not tell the whole story of how the little blind god played the rôle of fireman and took a hand in the preservation of the Van Steenburgh rooftree. A widow of engaging manners, then living in the house, so the story goes, had met a number of the British officers while on a visit to New York City some months previously. As luck would have it, the officer commanding the detachment detailed to fire that part of Kingston where the Van Steenburgh house stood had been deeply smitten by the widow's charms. At her entreaties, he promised to spare her home, but added that, by way of precaution, it would be well to display the British flag prominently. Thereupon, when the work of destruction began, the fair widow climbed to the roof and from this lofty perch waved the flag, or her red flannel petticoat as some aver, over her safe abode while her neighbours' houses crackled and burned. Fortunately, the old Dutch houses were so stoutly put together that the fire wrought but comparatively small damage. This was soon repaired and, consequently, the town preserves even now much of its colonial appearance.

Before Kingston got its charter as "Wiltwyck," the Dutch Reformed Church had its beginnings, and a very important part it played in the lives of the townspeople thence onward. Dominie Hermanus Blom came in 1659 and ministered faithfully until 1667, after which there was no regular pastor for eleven years. In 1678 came Dominie Van Gaasbeek, and the following year the congregation built a new stone church, 45 by 60 feet in size, which they say was elaborately finished and had stained glass windows with armorial bearings blasoned in them. Sunday observance and universal church-going were considered cardinal obligations. Nevertheless, human frailties came in for some allowance. At weekday prayer-meetings, commonly held from house to house, both spiritual and spirituous comfort were usually dispensed alike. One instance is recorded where a certain member of the congregation asked the Dominie to excuse him from having the meeting in his turn because he couldn't afford to pay for the drinks!

One bibulous affair connected with the church deserves to be chronicled for its human spontaneity:

"At the burning of Kingston the old church bell was destroyed. Some years later Colonel Henry Rutgers presented the congregation with a ship's bell to hang in the steeple. But it didn't sound right. It had a profane tone and reminded the town fathers of the ships' bells they had heard on the British men-of-war in New York Harbour or, what was even worse, of the ships' bells they had heard right in their own part of the river when Sir James Wallace brought General Sir John Vaughan to burn Kingston. It was plain that another bell must be obtained. But where should they get one? They imported their dominies from Holland, so why not import a bell thence, too? This, after proper deliberation, they decided to do. In due time, in the year 1794, the bell, a 'genuine Holland Amsterdam bell,' arrived accompanied by a very pious letter, all in dignified Dutch, from the bell founder, one Paulus Kuk, who prays 'that when on the day of rest she [the bell] lets her voice be heard, the congregation may diligently come up to the House of the Lord to hear His word and to make needful use of it.'

Alack, and alas! The good people were doomed to bitter disappointment. The bell was hung, but when they went to ring it, it would give out only a weak and dish-panny note. They had been buncoed. The 'genuine Holland Amsterdam bell,' after all was no better than an old cow-bell, and Paulus Kuk, despite all his pious protestations, was a fraud. In righteous wrath they were about to pack their troublesome purchase back to Holland, when Colonel Rutgers again came to the rescue with some timely suggestions about hanging. They followed his advice, and lo! the bell gave forth a beautifully strong, clear tone. Wrath gave place to joy, and so exuberant was their delight that they brewed gallons of punch, good old Dutch punch, and drank it—that's what it was for, to be sure—drank every bit of it and, so tradition has it, Dominie and people reeled on the sidewalk and rolled in the gutter, and some of the flock even got locked in the church over night by accident. They all had a royal good time while the punch lasted and were none the worse for it afterwards. If anyone with an overdeveloped sense of decorum is disposed to censure this merry little outburst of spirits, it is just as well they should remember that some punches that look quite harmless have a direfully insidious way about them that sets heads and heels topsy-turvy."

The Constitution of the State of New York, finally adopted April 20, 1777, was proclaimed from the steps of Kingston Courthouse. It has always been held that the Constitution was draughted in the old "SENATE HOUSE" (Plate 154), for it was there John Jay had his rooms and did most of his writing. It was in this house also that the Senate of New York held its sessions until the sittings of the Legislature were suspended because the British forces were approaching. The "Senate House" so called, built about 1678, was used by the State Senate because there was no room for them in the Courthouse. The "Senate House" was really the Ten Broeck house, but has long been called by its present name. Major (afterwards General) John Armstrong, of "Newburgh Letters" fame, lived there for some time while his children were being educated in Kingston. Aaron Burr, likewise, is said to have lived or visited there on one or more occasions, and those who de-

PLATE 159   TAPPEN HOUSE, KINGSTON: WEST FRONT   NO. 92 ON MAP

PLATE 160   TJERCK DE WITT HOUSE, ON ROAD TO OLD HURLEY: NO. 93 ON MAP
                              VIEW FROM SOUTHEAST

light in such eerie things profess to have heard his ghost on summer evenings playing the violin softly in one of the upper rooms. The house is a long, low, one-and-a-half storey structure, with an extension at the rear, built of the native bluish limestone in the typical early Dutch manner. It is now a museum of local history.

Another house, said to be even older than the "Senate House," is the HOFFMANN HOUSE (Plate 156), on North Front Street, near one of the old town gates. Tradition says it was built, or a part of it, in 1658. It is believed to have done duty as a fort more than once and, according to local report, was the scene of a massacre. Much more agreeable is the recollection of a later incident. It is said that when the Hoffmann family were living there, during the Revolution, a daughter of the family was sitting on the *stoep* at the house-door. It was one of the times when Washington was in Kingston. The Commander-in-Chief, with his staff, was riding past the house; the glances of the young officers were too much for the maiden who precipitately fled indoors disclosing, as she went, a well-turned ankle. *"My God, what an ankle!"* exclaimed Washington, always quick to perceive and appreciate feminine charms. The house is massively built of native stone, with unusually thick walls—quite thick enough to have answered for a fort—and flooring boards, or rather planks, often more than 15 inches wide. There seems to be no particular plan and the rooms are at all different levels so that it is hard to tell at any point whether you are upstairs or down. The place is now the local Salvation Army Headquarters, and the exterior walls are covered with a brownish red wash.

The VAN BUREN HOUSE (Plate 157), at Maiden Lane and John Street, is an edifying example of intelligent restoration—a visible assurance of what could readily be done not only with old Dutch stone houses in the immediate neighbourhood of Kingston that have suffered inconsiderate treatment from "improvers" in recently-past generations, but also with all the old houses of Dutch, or mixed Dutch and English, lineage on both sides of the Hudson. It is an object lesson that may well inspire widespread emulation; it ought certainly to stimulate appreciation of the Hudson Valley's priceless architectural heritage and the possibilities it holds.

The Sleght or TAPPEN HOUSE (Plate 159), where Crown and Green Streets merge, is now the local headquarters of the Daughters of the Revolution and is preserved in admirable condition. The building is much older than it looks and dates from long before the Revolutionary War. Its associations, however, are largely with the Revolutionary period and the names of General Washington, Governour Clinton, the Tappens, Sleghts and Wynkoops are closely connected with it. In the early 19th century a book and stationery shop was kept there and the *Ulster Plebeian* was published on the premises.

The DE WITT HOUSE (Plate 160), *"betwixt Hurley and Kingston,"* dates from about 1670, that is, the oldest part at the south end does. The house has grown to its present dimensions by successive additions; the second part at the south end was added early in the 18th century, it seems, while the whole northern end was built about 1799. The first part of the house was built by Tjerck Claessen De Witt who came to New Netherland in 1657 and went to Beverwyck (Albany); thence he removed to "Wiltwyck" in 1660 or 1661. In 1669-70 Governour Sir Francis Lovelace granted him permission to *"erect a house and barne with convenient outhouses for his cattle upon his own land at Esopus, lying betwixt Hurley and Kingston,"* the land previously granted him by Governour Nicoll; this was apparently a concession made in view of the former regulation (already mentioned) against building farmsteads in the open country, although Hurley is only about 3 miles to the westward of Kingston.

Old Hurley is Dutch in everything but name, and that was Dutch for the first few years of its history when it was Nieuw Dorp, that is, New Village. With characteristically Dutch conservatism, Old Hurley has slumbered on through its nearly three centuries of existence; tucked away, as it were, in a backwater past which the swirling eddies of modern progress have raced heedless of its presence, it has preserved a refreshing savour of the days and ways of the New Netherland of Pieter Stuyvesant. Hurley cheeses and the Kingston refugees of 1777 have given Hurley most of its renown in the outside world. So plentiful and so famous once were the former that Hurley was credited with "cheesemines." Kingston folk highly esteemed the "pot cheese" of Hurley and there was a brisk trade in this toothsome commodity. In time, Pot Cheese became synonymous with Hurley, and with gentle derision Kingston citizens would allude to Hurleyites as "pot-cheesers," or greet them with a jingle that ran:

"Some come from Hurley, some from the Rhine;
Some pop fresh from a Pot Cheese Mine."

This Kingstonian pleasantry the people at Hurley did not keenly relish. The following old Dutch verses, done into English by a local antiquary, tell of plenty at Old Hurley, not only of pot cheese but of many other good things as well:

PLATE 161   VAN DEUSEN HOUSE, OLD HURLEY: WEST FRONT   NO. 94 ON MAP

PLATE 162   VAN DEUSEN HOUSE, OLD HURLEY: VIEW FROM SOUTHEAST

PLATE 163   TEN EYCK HOUSE, OLD HURLEY: EAST FRONT   No. 97 ON MAP

PLATE 164   OLD GUARD HOUSE, OLD HURLEY: WEST FRONT   No. 96 ON MAP

PLATE 165   ELMENDORF HOUSE, OLD HURLEY: WEST FRONT   No. 95 ON MAP

"What shall we with the wheat bread do?"
    "Eat it with cheese from Hurley."
"What shall we with the pancakes do?"
    "Dip them in the syrup of Hurley."
"What shall we with the cornmeal do,
    That comes from round about Hurley?"
"Johnnycake bake, both sweet and brown,
    With green cream cheese from Hurley."

The old Dutch, indeed, sounds realistic with the question, *"Wat zullen wij met die pannekoeken doen?"*; at the answer, *"Doop het met die stroop van Horley,"* one involuntarily licks his chops over the dripping sweetness of *"die stroop."*

Comfort, solid comfort, is the keynote of Hurley indoors and out. Its houses, built along the one village street, their farm lands stretching back beyond them, have a convincing aspect of substantial prosperity and cheer. Long, low buildings they are, with thick stone walls, many of their upper gable-ends weather-boarded. Their roofs, jutting just above the windows of the ground floor, enclose within their shingled slopes great, roomy garrets that seem like very Noah's Arks, where everything under the sun was stowed in their cavernous recesses. Such part of this upper region as the old Dutchmen could spare from storage purposes, they made into chambers for their increasing families, and pierced the roof slope with tiny dormers. Oftentimes, however, the only light came in at the gable-ends through windows on each side of the massive chimneys. It was not at all unusual to give the whole attic storey to the storage of grain and other farm products, while the family lived altogether on the ground floor, their sleeping rooms opening off in unexpected places from the rooms of general use. Often one gable-end had a broad door in the attic, and a projecting beam and pulley above it to hoist bulky articles from outside. Curiously enough, grain was very commonly stored in casks and hogsheads. Cellars were not one whit behind attics in capacity for holding supplies. New Netherlanders were valiant trenchermen before whose eyes the pleasures of the table loomed large, and they consumed an amazing lot of victuals. Such overflowing store of potatoes and carrots, turnips, pumpkins and apples as went into those capacious bins! Rolliches and head cheeses were there, with sausages, scrapple, pickles, preserves and jams, to say nothing of barrels of cyder. These all contributed their share to that elusively complex odour of plenty that rose through the chinks of the floor and pervaded the rooms above. Only those who have met them face to face, in all their substantial corporeality, can realise the indescribable cellar smells of old Dutch farmhouses.

In May, 1662, on a part of the Esopus lands, a company from Beverwyck started a settlement. This was the beginning of Nieuw Dorp. The following spring, the settlers and agents of the Beverwyck

syndicate were so prospering and so busy tilling the soil that they disregarded warnings of danger from the Indians. Heedless of the order that a guard should be set when the men were working in the fields, each man was intent on cultivating his own land with a will. On June 7, 1663, the savages, inflamed by contraband rum, burst suddenly on the settlement with fire and tomahawk. Everyone was taken unawares; there was no chance to resist. It was all over in a twinkling. The village was in ashes, three men had been killed, and one man, eight women and twenty-six children carried away captive. Amongst the latter were the wife and three children of Louis du Bois; this ultimately led to the planting of a new settlement (New Paltz) in the Walkill Valley, as will appear later. Fortunately, the captives were not harshly treated and were all eventually recovered. The Indians who had made this raid soon came to terms; before long Nieuw Dorp village was rebuilt, and the settlers were again tilling their lands in peace. It was not, however, until several years later, when New Netherland had become·the Province of New York, that the village got a really good second start in life. The lands were re-surveyed, conflicting claims adjusted, and Governour Sir Francis Lovelace renamed the place Hurley, after Hurley-on-Thames, the Berkshire seat of his family. Thenceforth, despite wars and rumours of wars, Hurley lived peacefully on in its retired nook and prospered, with little exciting interruption, save for the brief flurry at the time of the Revolutionary War when all of Hurley's days of excitement came close together—the arrival of Cadwallader Colden, junior, to live under parole at CAPTAIN JAN VAN DEUSEN'S HOUSE (Plate 161); the descent of the Kingston refugees; the encampment of General Clinton's troops and the hanging of Lieutenant Daniel Taylor as a spy; the sitting of the Council of Safety, until the cold weather drove them away; and, towards the end of the war, General Washington's visit on one of his progresses, when he stopped at the village long enough to receive an address of welcome.

Cadwallader Colden, junior, son of a former Lieutenant-Governour of the Province, was a Loyalist; though he took no active sides in the political troubles, the excited Whigs of New Windsor and Newburgh adjudged him a dangerous person and had him confined in the Fleet Prison at Kingston. In September, 1777, he was released on parole and sent to live at Hurley. The oath he had to take reads:

"I, Cadwallader Colden Esq., Do Solemnly Promise unto Charles De Witt & Gouverneur Morris, a Committee of the Councill of Safety . . . upon my Enlargement from the fleet Prison, That I will forthwith Repair to the House of Cap'n Van Deusen, at Hurley, and will not go more than two miles

PLATE 166   HOUGHTALING HOUSE, OLD HURLEY: VIEW FROM NORTHWEST   NO. 98 ON MAP

PLATE 167   "SALLY TACK TAVERN" (MRS. E. C. CHADBOURNE'S HOUSE),   No. 99 ON MAP
STONE RIDGE: SOUTH FRONT

from said House without the Permission of his Excellency George Clinton Esq. the gov'r of the said state. . . ."

Before General Sir John Vaughan set fire to Kingston, October 16, 1777, the townspeople had seen the British fleet in the river and well knew they would be attacked. They also knew that Governour Clinton's troops could not get to Kingston in time to oppose any resistance. Prompt flight was the only course they had. Along the road to the west streamed a scurrying, motley procession of people, cattle, pigs, pack animals and waggons laden with poultry, farm implements, and such household effects and valuables as a hasty flight allowed them to collect. To plentiful, prosperous, cheese-making Hurley they went, and were received with open arms, fed and sheltered, though the coming of so many refugees sorely taxed the resources of the village. Governour Clinton's forces, about 1000 strong, arrived the 17th, the day after Kingston was burned —and they, too, were welcomed and fed, and lay there encamped for some time.

While in Hurley, Governour Clinton made his headquarters at Van Sickel's Tavern. This hostelry,

from the day it was built early in the 18th century, till its destruction by fire in the 20th, was always an inn and had one of the longest continuous licenses as a public house in the country. From the bough of an apple tree behind the inn they hanged Lieutenant Taylor, the full story of whose capture and trial belongs to New Windsor. The haste of leaving New Windsor and the rapid march, first to Marbletown and then on to Hurley, had prevented an earlier execution of the sentence, although the Governour had approved the court-martial's finding and signed the death warrant. On the way from New Windsor, the prisoner

"had a long, thin rope around his neck, which was coiled and carried after him by a soldier. On halting at Marbletown he was led into the church, then used as a depôt, and being seated near the pulpit the poor wretch bent himself forward to hide his face, and the rope was then coiled upon his back."

On the morning of the 18th the troops were paraded behind the tavern, Taylor was brought from his place of confinement (now known as the OLD GUARD HOUSE, Plate 164), made to stand on top of a hogs-

PLATE 168   FORMER DUTCH REFORMED PARSONAGE, STONE RIDGE: No. 100 on Map
                            VIEW FROM NORTHWEST

head, the rope was made fast to the apple tree bough, and then a soldier kicked the hogshead from under. As a reward for his grisly job, the executioner got the dead officer's boots. In a manuscript journal kept by a parson in Clinton's force, apparently a chaplain, is this entry:

"October 18th, Saturday. Mr. Taylor, a spy taken in Little Britain, was hung here. Mr. Romain and myself attended him yesterday, and I have spent the morning in discoursing to him, and attended him at the gallows. He did not appear to be either a political or a gospel penitent."

Small wonder that emetics, coiled ropes, lengthy exhortations and the sundry gentle attentions of an hostile soldiery failed to produce conversion to a political creed which he honestly believed to be rebellion! They buried him under a flagstone before the inn door. All this spectacle the townspeople and the Kingston refugees did not miss; it was ever after one of the outstanding events in Hurley's history.

Hurley now became the State's capital for a season. On November 18th the Council of Safety, which had fled from Kingston to Marbletown and sat there in the interval, moved to Hurley and held their sessions in Captain Van Deusen's house. The weather soon got so cold that the members suffered greatly. They paid "Cornelius Duboys" twenty shillings

"for collecting the parts of a stove, belonging to, or used by the late Convention of this State, from the ruins of the courthouse and gaol at Kingston, and transporting the same to Hurley," but "The experience of that stove had so warped its judgment and nature that it was no longer the genial giver of warmth,"

and the Councillors, with blue noses and chattering teeth, were literally frozen out and forced to vacate the premises. After ordering Captain Van Deusen to be paid

"the sum of thirty dollars in full for the use of his room and firewood, and other services for this Council,"

the refrigerated executives adjourned to Poughkeepsie and the old house dropped back into the somnolence of village humdrum.

Hurley had its taste of witchcraft, though not a serious incident. In the ELMENDORF HOUSE (Plate 165), once a tavern, there was long kept the

"visible evidence that witches did exist at Hurley. It seems that a witch once got into the churn and the butter would not come. Now the cure for this is a red hot horseshoe dropped into the refractory cream, and this method was adopted with entire success, the horseshoe being so thoroughly heated that the cream had not entirely cooled its ardour by the time it reached the bottom of the churn, where was left its faint imprint. The churn was so well exorcised that never again did the witch venture within."

The last immediate thrill of excitement Hurley had in the Revolutionary War was when General Washington, in 1782, passed through the town on his way to Kingston. It was a cold, rainy November day. As the cavalcade reached the corner where the Kingston road leaves the village street, his Excellency was halted in front of the HOUGHTALING HOUSE (Plate 166), then an inn, to hearken to the Chief Burgess read *"The Humble Address of the Trustees of the Freeholders and Inhabitants of the Town of Hurley, to His Excellency George Washington, General and Commander-in-Chief of the American Army."* The Chief Burgess was Matthew Ten Eyck, who lived in the comfortable TEN EYCK HOUSE (Plate 163) a little way up the street, now completely repaired and reconditioned by the present owner, Mr. Henry Morehouse. While the magistrate read this welcome from a dry shelter, the distinguished visitor sat on his horse listening, hat in hand, with his usual *savoir faire*, the raindrops trickling down his face, outwardly serene, but doubtless inwardly swearing, for Washington could swear upon occasion and did. It is pleasant to note that a glass of wine was brought out and offered his Excellency, so that not all the dampness was without. According to another local tradition, several small boys, advantageously posted on a fence opposite, blew a salute on pumpkin-vine trombones. Their efforts so amused and pleased the General that he called them into the tavern and gave them each a taste of wine from his glass. Whether the ambitious juvenile performance of pumpkin music really brought a vinous reward it is impossible to say but, at any rate, it seems reasonably certain that the General got some comfort to sustain him on his way to Kingston.

Stone Ridge, a few miles to the southwest of Old Hurley, is another village of similar character. One of the most engaging houses there is what is known as the SALLY TACK TAVERN (Plate 167), though now a private dwelling owned and occupied by Mrs. E. C. Chadbourne, who has put it in perfect condition, made some necessary enlargements at the back, and gathered within its walls an exceptionally choice and varied collection of all manner of Americana. It is said the house was built either by Jacobus Tack, whose marriage is recorded in 1727, or by his son Johannes. Johannes or John, it seems more likely, was the builder; the house has two full storeys, with an attic above, a type more to be expected later in the 18th century rather than during the prime of the elder Tack's life. In any case, the house was an inn for a number of years before the Revolutionary War. It served for a while as the meeting place of the first Ulster County Court, which County Judge Levi Pawling organised there May 5, 1778, after the establishment of the State Government. When Johannes Tack died, his widow took charge in 1790

PLATE 169   LONG WHITEWASHED HOUSE, STONE RIDGE: WEST FRONT   NO. 101 ON MAP

PLATE 170   THE LIBRARY, STONE RIDGE: SOUTH FRONT   NO. 102 ON MAP

and conducted the hostelry—hence the name, Sally Tack Tavern.

Across the road from the erstwhile Sally Tack Tavern is the Wynkoop-Lounsberry house, the home of Major Cornelius Wynkoop when General Washington spent the night there, November 15, 1782, on his way to Kingston—a fine large gambrel-roofed stone house, with excellent interior woodwork. Other typical houses in the village particularly worthy of mention are a long WHITEWASHED STONE HOUSE (Plate 169) south of the highway, with a somewhat unusual and highly interesting distribution of window openings on the east side; on the north side of the village street, the LIBRARY (Plate 170), whose walls are a splendid and representative specimen of the local stone masonry; and the former DUTCH REFORMED PARSONAGE (Plate 168), now a tea-room but—so far as the exterior is concerned—in its original condition except for the addition of dormers.

The LEVI HASBROUCK HOUSE (Plate 171) at Modena, a suave example of sophisticated Regency or Federal Era elegance, seems worlds apart from the vigorous homespun simplicity of the Hasbrouck houses at New Paltz only a few miles away. Yet they were built only about a century apart in time, and by members of the same family. The Modena house is, so to speak, a milestone indicative of the march of prosperity, manners, tastes and mental outlook in the region. The contrast affords ground for thought.

The story of New Paltz might well be entitled "The Annals of a Quiet Village." Although the alarums of war have now and again startled its people, the immediate village has led a singularly peaceful existence; since its settlement in the latter part of the 17th century, the years have passed, punctuated only by Sundays and Church feast-days, with the usual village gatherings, and the usual courtings and matchmakings from which, in due time, the village Dominie reaped his profits on occasion of weddings.

In many ways New Paltz resembles Old Hurley only, if anything, it is more perfect in its 17th-century aspect, although surrounded on all sides by modernism. Old Hurley has stood still, and such few changes as have been wrought have taken place in the village itself. New Paltz, on the other hand has grown, but the growth has gone on round about and outside the old Huguenot settlement and left it almost untouched, so that the one original village street presents to-day much the same appearance it did more than two hundred years ago.

The settlement of New Paltz came about through the early misfortune that befell Old Hurley. When the Indians fell upon Hurley in 1663, burned the houses and carried away captive a number of the inhabitants, the wife and children of Colonel Louis du Bois, as already mentioned, were amongst those taken prisoner. In the rescue party that immediately set out on the trail of the marauders was Colonel du Bois and, as he passed through the country, he noted the fertile lands and plentiful streams of the Walkill Valley, where New Paltz now stands. Fortunate in getting back his wife and children, along with the other returned captives, so that they could make a fresh start at Old Hurley, Colonel du Bois, nevertheless, remembered the fair grounds he had traversed and it was not long before he, Abraham Hasbrouck and several others of that number of Huguenots who had taken refuge under the Dutch flag, sought permission to purchase land of the Indians and make settlements. The Indian deeds of sale are dated April 28 and May 26, 1677, while the letters patent, bearing confirmation of the grant and signed by Governour Sir Edmund Andros, bear date September 29, 1677. Colonel du Bois was leader of the settlement. The eleven heads of families who came hither from the neighbourhood of Old Hurley were nearly all related one to another. From Kingston the little party came in three carts to New Paltz, and the place where they encamped, about a mile south of the village, still bears the name "Tri Cor," which means in English "Three Carts." Tradition has it that when they alighted from the carts, one of the party read for them the 37th Psalm.

About 30 years after the first settlement, the substantial stone houses we see to-day began to replace the rude huts of the pioneers. The little street, appropriately enough, is called Huguenot Street. At the south end of it, on the west side, is the JEAN HASBROUCK HOUSE (Plate 172), built in 1712 (now a local history museum). Next is the DU BOIS HOUSE (Plate 175), built in 1705. This house has undergone some alterations, with the addition of verandahs, but one can still see the loopholes on the street front, contrived for defense in case of Indian violence. Over against it is the BEVIER-ELTINGE HOUSE (Plate 173), built in 1698, once a store, between which and the other mercantile establishment at the foot of the street, kept by the Hasbroucks, there was sharp rivalry. At the top of the street, built in 1720, is the HOUSE OF HUGUES FREER (Plate 174), one of the original Patentees, while nearby on the same side of the street is ABRAHAM HASBROUCK'S HOUSE (Plate 176), built in 1712, which boasts a secret room and, as the roadside marker reminds us, afforded a place for cock-fights in its kitchen.

Although the people led quiet, orderly lives, for the most part undisturbed by the doings of the world about them, they were far from dwelling in rustic crudeness. As early as 1699 they were sufficiently attentive to social refinements to have regularly-

PLATE 173   BEVIER-ELTINGE HOUSE, NEW PALTZ: WEST FRONT   No. 104 on Map

PLATE 174   HUGUES FREER HOUSE, NEW PALTZ: WEST FRONT   No. 105 on Map

taught dressmakers. The articles of apprenticeship for Sara Freer are still in existence, according to which, upon the advice of her brother Hugues, she was bound to M. David Bonrepos and Blanche du Bois, his daughter-in-law, dressmaker. By the terms of this agreement, M. Bonrepos, the schoolmaster, and his daughter-in-law engaged to instruct the said Sara in the art of dressmaking,

> "to feed her, lodge her, and educate her in the fear of the Lord, and to furnish her with whatever shall be necessary, having regard to her habits and manner of bringing up."

While surrounded by the Dutch and on most friendly terms with them, it seems that none of the original Patentees, and not many of the immediate children, intermarried with their Batavian neighbours. For 50 years all the church records were kept in French; for the next 70 years, by which time the Dutch leaven had penetrated the Huguenot settlement, the records were kept in Dutch. After that, English was used. The New Paltz people had their own schoolmaster, their own customs and, what was much more remarkable, their own systems of land tenure and legal administration. They were, to all intents and purposes, an independent, self-governing body, actually an *imperium in imperio,* recognised and respected so long as the Colonies remained under the British Crown, and permitted for some years after the Revolutionary War until, in 1785, the town was incorporated in the State Government and, by special act of Legislature, the grants and partitions of the ancient local government were confirmed.

This little democracy was known as the Government of the Dusine, or Twelve Men. It was really government by Parish Council, consisting of the twelve heads of families. These twelve men were chosen annually, and had power to act and *"set in order and unity all common affairs."* By common consent these twelve men were entrusted with power to divide the lands by lot within the New Paltz Patent, and they gave title thereto by word of mouth without written deeds. They also made rules with reference to the building of fences, and imposed fines for the violation of these rules. Such exercise of judicial power as there was, likewise resided in their hands, and it does not appear that any appeal from the acts of the Dusine was ever carried to the Colonial Government. Besides the Dusine, there were regularly chosen town officers with varied duties. The members of the Dusine were descendants in either the male or female line from the original Patentees whom they represented, and were chosen by a *viva voce* vote at the annual election meetings. This curious little patriarchal oligarchy has no parallel in the colonial history of America.

Albeit the people of New Paltz spent uneventful lives and kept much to themselves, they took their own wholesome share in the sports of the day. Foot-racing, cock-fighting, horse-racing and, in winter, skating furnished amusement and excitement for the young and sometimes for the old as well. They tell the story of one young wag who got even with Dominie Bogardus—a son of that more famous Dominie Bogardus of New Amsterdam—for a reproof the Dominie had administered, but a reproof not relished by the recipient. One day the Dominie was invited by the young blade to ride, and was given a horse that was accustomed to race at a certain place. As the Dominie approached this spot a confederate flicked the horse with a whip, and the other horses in company all started down their wonted course at the top of their speed; the Dominie was utterly unable to hold in his mount. By common consent, his horse was allowed to get ahead, and when it reached the goal, where others in the secret were already waiting, a jubilant shout went up, *"Hurrah for the Dominie!"* It was commonly said in the early days that when a young man went wooing, the gentle object of his attentions never thought of enquiring whether he would get drunk, but simply whether he was *ugly* when drunk.

Near Marlborough, between the highway and the river, is the MILL HOUSE (Plate 177). Just where an old and much-travelled Indian trail crossed a stream, in 1714 Gomez the Jew built his house, with unerring instinct for posting himself on a natural trade route where he could intercept the current of whatever profit flowed past his door. He knew the red men frequenting this trail usually had furs to barter. He wished to be where he could get the first pick of whatever the Indians had when they came down from the hill country to the north and west, before other traders could enter into competition.

Gomez built his house of stone with immensely thick walls. Like many of the other early dwellings of the region, it was of one storey, with a huge stone fireplace at each end, and a capacious garret overhead. Inside the house he had one large trading room and two smaller rooms, in one of which he stored his furs, while in the other he kept his beads. Some of these beads have been found in the garden. Gomez prospered exceedingly in the fur trade. As his means increased, he sent his peltries in his own ships to Spain and Portugal. At the time of his death, he was one of the wealthiest merchants in New York City and much respected by his fellow citizens. The memory of his presence in the neighbourhood is preserved by the name of the little stream running past his door; it is called the "Jew's Creek."

In 1772 Wolfert Acker, a sturdy Dutch American, bought the place. He was a great-grandson of Jan Acker, one of the early Dutch settlers in New Netherland, and a grandson of the Wolfert Acker

whom Washington Irving immortalised in *Wolfert's Roost*. This same Wolfert Acker, of Mill House, organised and operated the first line of packets on the Hudson, and also one of the first ferries north of New York City. At the time of the Revolutionary War he was an active Whig and his house was frequently the meeting place for the Whig leaders in that part of the country. It was early in his ownership that Acker built the upper storey of brick on top of the lower storey of stone. For this addition, Acker's negro slaves made the bricks and tile on the spot; they used home-made moulds and fetched the clay from the banks of the Hudson. Acker lived until 1830 to enjoy his home by the banks of Jew's Creek. After Acker, the next owner of Mill House was Henry Armstrong, who came here with his bride to pass their honeymoon and stayed 60 years! Here he wrote his Civil War novel, *Rutledge*, laying many of the scenes in this very house.

A little to the north of Mill House and also east of the highway is MAPLE GROVE (Plate 178), built in 1757 by Colonel Lewis du Bois—a descendant of the Huguenot Patentee of New Paltz—on a 3000 acre tract he had from his father. Stoutly framed of heavy timbers and encased with clapboards, it was the first clapboarded house in Ulster County. The roof is truncated at the gable-ends, jerkin-head wise, as at the Headquarters in Newburgh. Barring the addition of a 19th-century verandah on the south front, and the substitution of large-paned sashes for the old multiple glazing, Maple Grove presents much the same appearance as when the Colonel lived there, surrounded by his family and a retinue of black slaves. Colonel du Bois's mode of life was not only patriarchially ample and comfortable, but elegant as well, according to the standards of the time. Maple Grove enjoyed the distinction of being the first house in the neighbourhood where a china dinner service was used, and curious housewives from the country round about came journeying to see this unwonted piece of luxury.

When the War for Independence came, Colonel du Bois had already won his spurs in the French and Indian War. During the Revolutionary struggle he was active in organising the local resources. Being a prominent person, and his anti-British sentiments and activities well known, when the British came up the Hudson in 1777 on their way to burn Kingston, Maple Grove, plainly visible from the river, got marked attention from the gunners on the men-of-war. They fired red hot cannon balls at it to set it afire. They failed, but the cannon balls were preserved and, for years afterwards, the children of the household, when they went into the attic to play on rainy days, rolled them back and forth along the floor to make thunder. They are now in the museum of the Historical Society in Newburgh. In this house was held the meeting of the Masonic Lodge that deleted Benedict Arnold's name from the rolls.

At the return of peace, Colonel du Bois took up again his wonted mode of life at Maple Grove, busied with managing and improving his estate. Negro slaves, of whom he had a number, did most of the Colonel's cultivation. They found life comfortable and happy, certainly more protected and care-free than after they were emancipated. Slavery was abolished by law in New York in 1827, but before that not a few masters had freed their negroes. Colonel du Bois was one of them. His old friend, Colonel Leveritch, who lived just across the river and also owned many blacks, came often to Maple Grove to spend a day or two. On one of these visits, so they say, when the two were comparing notes, Colonel du Bois opined that slave labour was not profitable and that they would find themselves in pocket if they freed their slaves and hired the necessary farm labourers.

"How is that?" said Colonel Leveritch.
"We plough our lands in the spring," said Colonel du Bois, "we raise our crops and fatten our hogs and then, in the autumn when the crops are all in, we kill the hogs, smoke the hams and bacon, and salt down a lot of pork. Then comes the winter, and the blacks have to be kept and looked after. The blacks did the work, it is true, but during the winter and spring they eat up all the results of their work, and we are no better off than we were before. And the same thing goes on in a circle, year after year."
"That's so," said Colonel Leveritch, "I never thought of it that way before."
"I'm going to free my slaves," said Colonel du Bois.

And he did. He had come to the same conclusion as had Isaac de Peyster Teller about the appetites of his "damned niggers." Freeing the slaves, however, was easier talked about than done. When the slaves, six months beforehand, were told they were going to be freed, there was much rejoicing. They were kept over the winter, and they all trooped off in high glee over their newly-acquired freedom. In the autumn, though, they all came straggling back. When the Colonel reminded them they were now free, they answered,

'they didn't know where to go, or couldn't get work, or had nowhere to sleep. In short, they couldn't take care of themselves.'

The long and short of it was that Colonel du Bois had to take care of them all another winter, willy-nilly. Even after the second exodus the following spring, a certain number stayed on in their new capacity as hirelings with some responsibility for their own welfare, and faithful servants they were.

PLATE 176   ABRAHAM HASBROUCK HOUSE, NEW PALTZ: WEST FRONT   No. 107 ON MAP

PLATE 177   MILL HOUSE, MARLBOROUGH: VIEW FROM SOUTHEAST   NO. 110 ON MAP

PLATE 178   MAPLE GROVE, MARLBOROUGH: VIEW FROM SOUTHWEST   NO. 109 ON MAP

ORANGE COUNTY

THE first part of the HASBROUCK HOUSE (Plate 179) at Newburgh, commonly known as WASHINGTON'S HEADQUARTERS, was built in 1727. Colonel Jonathan Hasbrouck greatly enlarged it in 1750; in 1770 he added the northern part. Colonel Hasbrouck died in 1780. His son Isaac with the rest of the family continued to live there. There General Washington made his headquarters from April 4, 1782 to August 18, 1783.

To the left of the west door is a parlour; this the General and Mrs. Washington used as a private sitting room. Behind this, opening into the *"room with seven doors and one window,"* was the General's private office. Next to this, at the northeast corner, was their bedroom. Washington used the *"room with seven doors and one window"* as a general place of meeting with his officers and for the transaction of official business. It frequently did duty as a dining hall, although there was an adjoining room where they often ate.

When Washington established his quarters at Newburgh, there was general confidence that Yorktown had virtually put an end to the war and that full and final peace was only a matter of time. Nevertheless, as Commander-in-Chief of the Army, Washington had to maintain his organisation in preparedness. There were internal difficulties, too—tardiness and apparent indifference of Congress; growing discontent of officers and men at their treatment by the Government; contentions and jealousies between the States; and numerous minor vexations and perplexities—so that Washington's position was not one of care-free idleness, however much social gaiety there may have been as the period of Newburgh and New Windsor encampments drew to a close. On May 10, 1782, less than a month after he had taken up quarters at Colonel Hasbrouck's, Washington received Sir Guy Carleton's letter about peace proceedings. Twelve days later, pleasure at prospective peace was dimmed by annoyance at Colonel Nicola's letter suggesting that Washington, aided by the army, seize supreme power and place a crown on his own head. In the Newburgh house Washington penned his indignant rejection of any such proposal. May 28th, the orders for the day announced

> "The Commander-in-Chief is happy in the opportunity of announcing to the army the birth of a Dauphin of France; and . . . is pleased to order a *feu de joie* on Thursday next."

August 10th came a letter from Sir Guy Carleton and Admiral Digby to acquaint Washington that *"negotiations for a general peace have already commenced at Paris."* Early in January, 1783, came news that the preliminary treaty of peace had been signed, but relief on that score was soon clouded by anxiety over the "Newburgh Letters" episode, when Washington's prompt action averted a national disaster. When word came, towards the end of March, that a general Treaty of Peace had been signed, Washington issued the following from the Newburgh Headquarters:

> "The Commander-in-Chief orders the cessation of hostilities, between the United States and the King of Great Britain; to be publicly proclaimed to-morrow at twelve . . .; and that the Proclamation . . . be read to-morrow evening at the head of every regiment and corps of the army; after which the Chaplains with the several brigades will render thanks to Almighty God for all His mercies, particularly for His overruling the wrath of man to His glory, and causing the rage of war to cease amongst the nations."

Even before this happy culmination, the discipline of the camp was inevitably somewhat relaxed, and *"the increased facilities for social intercourse were improved to the fullest extent."* All the principal officers entertained and at headquarters the "Court" of the camp surrounded Mrs. Washington.

Those who attended them, long remembered the dinners and suppers at headquarters. Dinner came at two or three o'clock, and both dinners and suppers were

> ". . . as plentiful as the country could supply, and as good as they could be made by Continental cooks. The repasts ended, French wines for our French allies and those who affected their tastes, and more substantial Madeira for Americans of the old school, circulated freely and were served in little silver mugs or goblets made in France for Washington's camp equipage. In the summer time, the guests soon withdrew from the table to the open grounds; but in the autumn the long evenings were frequently passed around the table, beside the blazing fire. On such occasions apples and hickory nuts mingled with the wine; and the amazing consumption of the former, by Washington and his staff, was a theme of boundless wonder to the French officers."

Washington occasionally had recourse to ingenious expedients to supply his table at Newburgh. Continental bills were often worthless and coin not always to be had. Once when the specie ran out, so did the supply of eggs at the same time. In his *History of Orange County,* Eager notes that if there was one eatable Washington preferred to all others it was eggs, and the army had consumed all the eggs produced and found in the neighbourhood. When one of Washington's Life Guards, part of whose duty it was to provide for the General's table, told him the desperate state of affairs in the provision department, Washington straightway wrote out an order on the Quartermaster-General for a butt of salt. He very well knew that just then salt was even scarcer than money. The Quartermaster's office was puzzled by the call for so much salt at headquarters;

PLATE 179   WASHINGTON'S HEADQUARTERS (JONATHAN HASBROUCK HOUSE),   NO. 111 ON MAP
NEWBURGH: WEST FRONT

PLATE 180   WASHINGTON'S HEADQUARTERS (JONATHAN HASBROUCK HOUSE),
NEWBURGH: WEST DOOR

nevertheless, it was conveyed thither by two yoke of oxen. Then notice was given out to the country people that salt would be exchanged for eggs at headquarters. This produced the desired effect; eggs suddenly became plentiful. When the army left Newburgh, there were still several casks of salt in the house unconsumed.

A few miles west of Newburgh, on the north side of the road to Monticello, is the Hill House (Plate 185), a comely brick structure of the mid-18th century, obviously Georgian in parentage but with such occasional evidences of individual interpretation as might be expected from local artisans untrained in the subtleties and precedents of Georgian detail. An instance of such interpretation, both naïve and ingenious, may been seen in the panelling (Plate 186) where Ionic capitals assume a form without recorded precedent but diverting through its unintended whimsicality.

On the north side of the same road, and a little nearer Newburgh, is what remains of Coldenham (Plate 187), the stone house of Cadwallader Colden. Its present sorry condition—both from extreme dilapidation and from the various architectural defacements to which it has been subjected through the years—calls for the exercise of considerable imagination to visualise the house as it was in the day of the Provincial Lieutenant-Governour and his son Cadwallader Colden junior. Both outside and in, it was a fine example of contemporary domestic architecture. The panelling of the interior has fortunately been preserved by transfer to the Metropolitan Museum in New York City.

The house known as the Knox Headquarters of New Windsor (Ellison house—Plate 188) is now kept as an historic landmark through the generosity of a few interested persons who presented it to the State. Major General Henry Knox occupied it on several occasions as his official residence while the American Army was encamped in the neighbourhood. Also, at sundry times, it sheltered other distinguished officers. The record of General Knox's occupancy is very explicit; it is a certificate signed by him, dated at West Point September 9, 1783, and states that he, General Greene, and Colonels Biddle and Wadsworth

"occupied three rooms, as military quarters, in Mr. John Ellison's house, five weeks in the months of June and July, 1779," and that "I, the subscriber, occupied three rooms as military quarters ten weeks in the fall of this year; also from the 20th of November, 1780, to the 4th of July, 1781, I occupied two rooms as military quarters; and from May, 1782, to September, I occupied one room, for the same purpose, making fourteen weeks."

General Knox's residence there lasted in all more than a year. During part of this time Mrs. Knox was

with him to grace the place and act as hostess, for wherever the Knoxes were there was sure to be hospitality and entertainment. Even in the darkest days of the American fortunes they managed to buoy the spirits of those around them. Most, if not all, of the distinguished American officers, as well as equally distinguished officers of the allies, often passed in and out of the door of this house while the portly General Knox and his scarcely less portly spouse—they were both "substantial" persons—were in residence there, stopping to chat and drink the health of their host and hostess in a glass of wine or a "thimbleful" of something more potent. In addition to being fond of entertaining, the Knoxes were exceptionally good conversationalists and wherever they were there was no dullness or lack of worthwhile talk. Their quarters

"seemed like a home in the midst of the camp and the officers were glad . . . to spend as much time there as possible. Time hung heavy on their hands; they had plenty of leisure to be social, and doubtless they availed themselves of every opportunity to relieve the monotony of their life in camp."

Mrs. Knox, from time to time *gave her choice soirées, graced by the presence of Mrs. Washington and other ladies of taste and refinement, with whom the region abounded.*" It was in this house, by accepted local tradition, that Washington opened a ball with Maria Colden for his partner. She was a relative of the Ellisons and, at that time, one of the most admired belles of Orange County. As a memento of this festivity, three of the young ladies scratched their names with a diamond on a window pane. The names, still legible, are Sally Jansen, Gitty Wynkoop and Maria Colden. Mrs. Knox did not confine her cheer-radiating efforts to the official circle; she was indefatigable in her ministrations to the welfare of the soldiers. It seems likely that she was at the New Windsor headquarters from November 1780 to July 1781; from certain allusions, it is almost certain she was there at other times, too.

There are other memories of Washington connected with the Ellison house than those of balls and soirées. There is reason to believe the tradition that he stopped there and, after some refreshment, rode on in company with several generals of his staff to the "New Building" or "The Temple" on that memorable meeting of the officers he had convened there because of the anonymous addresses circulated in the camp counselling drastic measures to bring Congress to terms—the addresses known as the "Newburgh Letters."

"General Gates presided. Washington took his station at the desk, drew from his coat a written address and, lifting his spectacles to his eyes, remarked:—'Gentlemen, you will permit me to put on my spectacles, for I have not only grown grey, but almost blind in the service of my country.' Eyes were everywhere suffused with tears and the meeting was at the sway of its commander."

PLATE 181　　　　　WASHINGTON'S HEADQUARTERS (JONATHAN HASBROUCK HOUSE),
NEWBURGH: RIVER FRONT

The old weather-boarded part of the house was built in 1734. In 1754, Thomas Ellison, who was living in the house that Washington subsequently used as his New Windsor headquarters, built the stone addition for his son John. The stone structure thenceforth became the main part of the house; the earlier part was given over altogether to the kitchens and servants. Tradition in the Ellison family says that the original wooden part of the house was built by Thomas Ellison for the slaves who took care of his hunting dogs and looked after the extensive tract of land on which the building stood. In the stone part is a "witch's stair" to the attic, ingenious but not comfortable. In the former panelled parlour (now the dining-room—Plate 190) General Knox is believed to have discussed informally the formation

PLATE 182   WASHINGTON'S HEADQUARTERS (JONATHAN HASBROUCK HOUSE), NEWBURGH: PARLOUR

of the Society of the Cincinnati. It is likely, therefore, that this room may be credited with the conception of the Society afterwards fully organised at Mount Gulian.

Between New Windsor and Cornwall-on-Hudson, just north of the mouth of Moodna Creek, PLUM POINT (Plate 191) stands on a high promontory overlooking the river. Built by Philip Verplanck in 1834, on land he had bought from John Dowden Nicoll, at the height of the Greek Revival, Plum Point is an outstanding example of the adaptation of Greek temple design to domestic architecture with its stately Doric hexastyle porticoes extending across the east and west fronts. During the Revolutionary War a *chevaux-de-frise* was stretched from the shore at this place to Pollopell's Island, and Machin's Battery formed a part of the river defense system. The breastworks of the battery are still visible.

Just south of Plum Point, its lands bordered by the Moodna Creek and Hudson River, is the NICOLL FARMHOUSE (Plate 192), built in 1735. The house is near, or perhaps on the very spot, where the leader of the first white colonists in what is now Orange County, Captain Patrick McGregorie, built his cabin in 1685. Always in the forefront as pioneers the world over, Scots have lent a distinctly Caledonian flavour to the planting of Orange County.

Dr. John Nicoll * of New York City—one of the four founders of the First Presbyterian Church, in Wall Street (1719), who purchased the "de Peyster Garden" and gave it for the church site—in the

---

* Dr. Nicoll was cited for special commendation by the General Assembly of the Church of Scotland and it was said of him, "while a Presbyterian Church subsists in the City of New York, the name of Nicoll will ever be remembered with honour, as one of its principal founders and its greatest benefactor." Dr. Nicoll was born in Edinburgh in 1684, came to New York in 1711, and died there in 1743.

PLATE 183   WASHINGTON'S HEADQUARTERS (JONATHAN HASBROUCK HOUSE),
                   NEWBURGH: THE "ROOM WITH SEVEN DOORS AND ONE WINDOW"

PLATE 184   WASHINGTON'S HEADQUARTERS (JONATHAN HASBROUCK HOUSE),
                   NEWBURGH: DINING ROOM

PLATE 185   HILL HOUSE, NEAR COLDENHAM: SOUTH FRONT   No. 113 ON MAP

PLATE 186   HILL HOUSE, NEAR COLDENHAM: PARLOUR

PLATE 187   COLDENHAM, AT COLDENHAM: SOUTH FRONT   No. 112 ON MAP

PLATE 189   Knox's Headquarters (Ellison House), New Windsor:
North Side

PLATE 190   Knox's Headquarters (Ellison House), New Windsor:
Former Parlour

autumn of 1734 bought a large tract fronting on the Hudson just above the mouth of the Moodna. This he turned over to his son, Dr. John Nicoll junior, who held his arts and medical degrees from the University of Edinburgh. It was this second John Nicoll who built the house the following year. From that day the Nicoll family has always been closely identified with the building of Orange County. Nicolls —and sometimes three Nicolls—have fought in every conflict since the French and Indian War (except the Spanish-American War) and are still doing so, in the eighth generation. At the time of the Revolutionary War, both John and Leonard Nicoll were members of the Committee of Safety (in 1777), and their brother Isaac was in command at Fort Constitution in 1776. During the encampment of the Continental Army at New Windsor, Dr. John Cochran, Surgeon-General and Director-General of Hospitals, made his headquarters in the Nicoll farmhouse and spent two winters there. General du Portail, commanding the army's Corps of Engineers, Sappers and Miners, also lived there for a time. Whether General Washington ever visited or stayed in the house is not definitely known, but there seems a likelihood he did.

In 1842, John Nicoll IV and his wife, Elizabeth Nicoll Woodhull, moved the family seat from the farmhouse to Linden, the large house they had just built on the hill to the northwest. Their great-granddaughter, Mrs. Gordon E. Wightman, is now returning to live in the old farmhouse—which has fortunately escaped all disfiguring change—a home instinct with the memories of generations who, in their several times, *without much heralding, have gone about the business of being good citizens and, with great faith, building a nation.*

To gratify the sensationalism of movie producers, and partly through the obstinacy of an owner, an Orange County house about which centred important historical associations was demolished in the 20th century. The FALLS HOUSE near New Windsor was deliberately and intentionally burned down; by prearranged understanding, the movie photographers set up their cameras and filmed the incident! The age of barbarism seems not yet past.

Thither for refuge, to the house of the Widow Falls, came the wife and children of Governour Clinton—they had been living near the river in New Windsor—when Forts Clinton and Montgomery fell October 6, 1777. Thither came Governour Clinton himself, making the house his headquarters during those few strenuous days when he was rallying the troops before hastening to Kingston, where it was expected the British would strike the next blow. At noon, October 10th, while Governour Clinton was still at the Falls house, an horseman rode up to the camp guard and, when challenged, replied, "*I am a friend and wish to see General Clinton.*" He was taken to General Clinton but, to his dismay, found the gentleman for whom he had asked was not *his* General Clinton. The stranger was Lieutenant Daniel Taylor, of Captain Stewart's Company, in the Ninth Regiment of the British Army, and the General Clinton he had expected to find was *Sir Henry* Clinton. He was an express messenger sent by Sir Henry with a despatch to General Burgoyne. When he had passed the Highlands, meeting troops in British uniform he imagined that Sir Henry's forces had moved forward and drew near the camp. The men were wearing captured British uniforms that had not yet been re-dyed blue and this deceived him. Discovering his fatal mistake, Taylor put his hand to his mouth and apparently swallowed something. This excited Governour Clinton's suspicion and he sent straightway for Dr. Moses Higby of Newburgh, then living nearby; at the Governour's orders, the doctor administered a powerful emetic. What ensued, Clinton told in his letter to the Council of Safety. At a court-martial held October 14th, presided over by Colonel Lewis du Bois, Taylor was convicted as a spy. The rest of Taylor's story has been told in the account of Old Hurley. His execution as a *spy* seems hardly justified by the facts connected with his arrest; a local historian states that letters found in Taylor's possession showed that he was from Kinderhook and had enlisted in the service of the King, a circumstance that may well have infused hostile animus into the court's decision.

While the army lay at Newburgh and New Windsor in 1782 and 1783, the house is said to have been filled by officers. One of them is believed to have been Major John Armstrong, author of the "Newburgh Letters." It is not unlikely that he wrote the letters in this house.

IDLEWILD (Plate 193), the former home of the poet Nathaniel P. Willis, the outstanding literary celebrity of the Hudson Valley in his day, stands on the verge of a deep glen to the north of Cornwall-on-Hudson. The house occupies the northeast angle of a lofty plateau overlooking the river and bounded at the south by the bold mass of Storm King. The old Dutch name, *Boter Berg* (Butter Hill) was changed to Storm King at Mr. Willis's instance, and his efforts widely affected the nomenclature of the whole region. Idlewild is a product of the romantic episode in American architecture when the influence of Sir Walter Scott's *Waverly Novels* inspired the "Hudson River Gothic" style in the 1840's. The house now belongs to Mrs. Charles Curie.

THE SUPERINTENDENT'S HOUSE (Plate 194) at West Point, built about 1820, admirably exempli-

fies the spacious suavity that characterised the domestic architecture of the Federal Era. Historically it is associated with all the eminent military men who have filled the post of Superintendent, General Robert E. Lee amongst others.

The OLD CADETS' CHAPEL (Plate 195), built in 1837, is a convincing evidence of the dignified clas-

sicism that dominated American building, whether during the Federal Era or the days of the more austere Greek Revival.

The OFFICER'S HOUSE (Plate 196) in the "Hudson River Gothic" manner is a perfect and unspoiled specimen of Andrew Jackson Downing's romanticism.

PLATE 192   NICOLL FARMHOUSE, NEW WINDSOR: SOUTH FRONT   No. 116 ON MAP

PLATE 193   IDLEWILD, FORMER HOME OF NATHANIEL P. WILLIS,   No. 117 ON MAP
                   CORNWALL-ON-HUDSON: SOUTH FRONT

PLATE 195   OLD CHAPEL, WEST POINT: SOUTH FRONT   No. 118 ON MAP

PLATE 196   "HUDSON RIVER GOTHIC" OFFICER'S HOUSE, WEST POINT: No. 120 ON MAP
EAST FRONT

(Courtesy of New York Historical Society)

PLATE 197   "TREASON HOUSE," WEST HAVERSTRAW: EAST FRONT   NO. 121 ON MAP

ROCKLAND COUNTY

NEAR Haverstraw, until recent years, stood a dwelling known as the "TREASON HOUSE" (Plate 197). At the time of the Revolutionary War it was the home of Joshua Hett Smith and was the scene in one act of that tragedy in which a British officer lost his life and an American General lost his honour.

It was from the door of this house that Arnold went to keep his rendezvous with Major André at the foot of Long Clove Mountain on the night of September 21, 1780. Thither, just before daybreak, Arnold led the ill-fated André; within these walls, in a room on the upper floor, during the morning of September 22nd, were consummated the plans for the betrayal of West Point and the undoing of American hopes.

Joshua Hett Smith was a barrister and a brother of Chief-Justice William Smith, of New York City. The family were widely known and highly respected, and of influential associations. It was obviously to Arnold's advantage to have the apparent help and countenance of Smith as a shield against suspicion. Whether Smith was a knave or a fool has never been really determined. If he was ignorant of the negotiations he was assisting, he was Arnold's

dupe and cats-paw. He had complaisantly taken his family to Fishkill to visit friends, and then returned to Beverly to get his further instructions from Arnold. The rest of the story, in all its details, is well known and need not be rehearsed.

After Smith's escape from detention and his removal to England, his house did not figure in public affairs until August of the following year. On the 20th, when the allied armies were crossing the Hudson at King's Ferry, General Washington made his headquarters there. Claude Blanchard notes in his Diary:

> "On the 21st the [French] army left Northcastle. In the evening I received orders from the general [Rochambeau] to carry a letter to General Washington, who was already on the other side of the North River. . . . General Washington was occupying Smith's house, famous owing to the fact that there André and Arnold had held their meeting. General Washington was taking tea; I took it with him."

Washington stayed there till the 25th, and then left for Yorktown.

Tappan still may boast, as may so many of the historic towns of the Hudson Valley, of its famous dwellings—the HOUSE WHERE MAJOR ANDRÉ WAS

205

PLATE 198   MAJOR ANDRÉ'S PLACE OF CONFINEMENT, TAPPAN: EAST FRONT   NO. 122 ON MAP

PLATE 199   WASHINGTON'S HEADQUARTERS (DE WINDT HOUSE), TAPPAN: NO. 123 ON MAP
SOUTHWEST FRONT

PLATE 200   WASHINGTON'S HEADQUARTERS (DE WINDT HOUSE), TAPPAN:
NORTHEAST FRONT

CONFINED (Plate 198) during the period of his trial, and the HEADQUARTERS OF GENERAL WASHINGTON (Plate 199). The old Dutch Church, alas, has gone and only these two remain as little shrines for students of Revolutionary history.

Major André's prison-house (the so-called 'Seventy-Six House), built in 1755, is now an inn, boasting an "enlarged and improved ball-room," and caters to furnishing light refreshments. From this house André was led to execution, October 2, 1780.

In 1932, at the 200th anniversary of Washington's birth, members of the Fraternity of Free and Accepted Masons of the State of New York bought and thoroughly restored the Washington Headquarters.

Built in 1700 by Daniel de Clark, leader of the Tappan Patentees, in 1746 the house passed into possession of John de Windt, a West Indian planter from the Island of St. Thomas, and was known as the de Windt house when Washington occupied it at sundry times during the Revolutionary War. It was here, in 1780, that the Commander-in-Chief approved the report of a board of General Officers condemning Major André to death as a spy. And it was here, upon the conclusion of peace in 1783, that Washington entertained General Sir Guy Carleton, the British Commander-in-Chief, when they met to arrange the evacuation of New York City by his Majesty's forces. The house is now maintained as an historic monument and is open to the public.

INDEX